WITHDRAWN

Praise of the Secular

STUDIES IN RELIGION AND CULTURE
Frank Burch Brown, Gary L. Ebersole, and Edith Wyschogrod, Editors

PRAISE of the SECULAR

Gabriel Vahanian

University of Virginia Press | *Charlottesville and London*

University of Virginia Press
© 2008 by the Rector and Visitors of the University of Virginia
All rights reserved
Printed in the United States of America on acid-free paper

First published 2008

9 8 7 6 5 4 3 2 1

LIBRARY OF CONGRESS CATALOGING-IN-PUBLICATION DATA

Vahanian, Gabriel, 1927–
   Praise of the secular / Gabriel Vahanian.
     p.   cm.   — (Studies in religion and culture)
   Includes bibliographical references and index.
   ISBN 978-0-8139-2701-5 (cloth : alk. paper) — ISBN 978-0-8139-2703-9 (e-book)
   1. Secularization (Theology)   I. Title.
   BT83.7.V34 2008
   261—dc22
                                                                 2007027660

Contents

In Memoriam Charles E. Winquist   vii
Preface   xi
Acknowledgments   xviii

INTRODUCTION   1

1. THEOLOGY AND THE SECULAR   11
   Religion as Vindication of the Secular   12
   Faith and the Adiaphoricity of the World   19
   Inklings of the Secular   30

2. NO GOD IS GOD: INCARNATION AND THE SECULAR   38
   Worlding the Word: Incarnation and the Christ   39
   Christ—Neither God Nor Man   52

3. FICTIONS OF FAITH   65
   An Ethic of the Unprecedented   65
   A Gratuitous Ethic   69

4. THE DEATH OF GOD AND THE AMBIGUITIES OF THE SECULAR   76
   The Religious Meaning of the Secular: Language and the Self   77
   Religion Denatured: Tillich's Underestimation of the Secular   82
   The Secular and Ellul's Overestimation of the Sacred   86
   Language and Rorty's Blind Spot   87

5. THE SECULAR AND THE DEREGULATION OF RELIGION   90
    Between Theocracy and Anarchy: From the Sacred to Utopia   91
    The Two Bodies of the Christ   94
    *Beyond Pluralism and Fundamentalism: A Bridge over a River
       without Banks*   97

6. WORLDING THE WORD: INCARNATION AND THE
    OTHERNESS OF TIME   104
    Dated—Not Outdated: Timing the Eternal   105
    Anachronistic Time and Eternal Now   114
    Ecce Homo   125

    EPILOGUE—THE TWO HANDS OF LANGUAGE: A SECULAR CHRIST   127

Notes   133
Index   149

In Memoriam

Charles E. Winquist (1944–2002)

> yours are the poems i do not write.
>
> In this at least we have got a bulge on death,
> silence, and the keenly musical light
>
> of sudden nothing . . . . la bocca mia "he
> kissed wholly trembling"
>
>   or so thought the lady.
>
> —E. E. Cummings

A fiction of faith, even a mirage come true, the secular is, for Charles Winquist's all-embracing theology, what transcends the dialectic of religion and culture, soon forming a pair with theology. Necessarily, it opens the trail of a language through which semantics and semiotics can at last commingle in a unified desire both transcending the dichotomies of the letter and the spirit, of the soul and the body, and as resilient to their fusion as it is to the confusion of the human and the divine. As profound as it is thick, the secular is deep enough to show nothing but its see-through surface, much like lips that give mouth to the body through which, coming into one's own, one yet no longer belongs to oneself. Inseparable from one another, theology and the secular are terms that represent different yet conniving corrugations of the surface of a language whose words seem to belong to incommensurable paradigmatic explorations of the real and its opacity. Seemingly acquiescing to Tillich's correlation of religion and culture, Charles Winquist radically departs from it. His correlation, by contrast, consists in an emphatic vindication of the secular, even if switching from one lexical game to another, from Tillich's condescending spiritualizing of the secular to his unadorned secularizing of the spiritual. Nevertheless, Winquist describes our secular situation as one of estrangement and dereliction. Sin and salvation seem still to be riding herd on the flocks of his language as if forgiveness had to do more with merits and their proliferating simulacra than with grace and its simulations of a naïveté never really lost unless and until it is regained. Winquist somehow continues to view the secular as a bruise on the surface of language, a birthmark on the skin of a culture more parricidal than actually come of age and, paradoxically, more obsessed with a tradition it rejects and on whose legacy it yet continues to lay claim. Why does Winquist need to be reminded that grace does not eclipse but calls for radical secularity?

The secular is to the theological as the topological is to the tropological or as the literal is to the metaphorical and, for Winquist, its paramount variant, metonymy. God is a symbol of God. From the natural to the symbolic there is, with Tillich, no need to switch gears. Not so with Winquist's metonymy; we must change gears as we move from the nonsymbolic statement about God as being-itself to what it actually stands for—the otherness of God—as we move from the natural to the cultural (or second-nature) naïveté of the symbol. Unlike Tillich's telluric thinking about the symbol, Winquist's secular approach reminds us that nothing is more symbolic than the literal, than the word that hits rock bottom all the way down to the lowest ring of language and, there, is as empty as a tomb. But because "our talk [is then] of a God that remains unspoken," "sometimes it cannot be written." But then again, rather than merely ecstatic, it is eschatic: Jesus indeed comes, not so much to "save" us as to proclaim the kingdom of God, the antidote to our obsession with salvation. This is a kingdom that is neither here nor there. Like Winquist's own discourse, it leaves us with nothing but the desirable, with that which both in its ultimate and in its intimate dimensions endures life, holding out to death throughout a lifetime, never coming into its own, except once and for all.

Desire, that most emblematic vocable of Winquist's, has no end; it is not marred with the obsession either of an end or of an ending. Having no object, it is all the more tortured by the thought of a God it refrains from objectifying, lest it should counterfeit itself. But this quest for purity, which Kierkegaard located in the heart, is by Winquist located in the body. The body exudes and at once begs for love—just as the secular exudes and, in dire need of faith, begs for it. A secular body, however, was also what ecclesia was meant to emulate. Ecclesia: a city without a temple, without a final vocabulary—only a text woven together out of a tongue nobody speaks, still short of a language and spared from its perversions and therefore set to "music for no instrument," as E. E. Cummings would say. It is a text so worlded and set to fall into place—if any—as would the poem itself, which, woven from all the "poems i do not write," would be worlding the word and yet build no temple. It blows a kiss, "a bulge on death." It worlds the word into "music for no instrument," into a body—a lady's or that of Christ, into a poem, which, not merely literal, let alone merely symbolic, would outlast death as desire would outlast itself and faith or a kiss outlast religion and its temples. No more necessary than contingent upon that which simply happens, worlding the word collapses that which would last forever into that which, at last universal as well as singular, would last once and for all. Likewise collapsing the ultimate and the intimate into one another, worlding the word gives mouth to a kiss—to a poem no word underwrites unless it becomes flesh, or so at least Charlie would think, along with E. E. Cummings's lady.

Preface

Rather than eviscerating religion, the secular has played a major role in prodding religion into overcoming itself. Instead of the religious showing the way to the secular, the secular is now what is showing the way to religion, whether in the sense of each pointing to, or of each giving way to, the other. In this light, what religions have in common is not the doctrines or dogmas that drive a wedge between them but the world, a world globalizing so fast that religions are no longer confined to their natural habitat. Like Athens and Jerusalem in the Roman Empire, the world that religions have in common is another name for the secular—and its yearning for a new type of religiosity, no longer restricted to our habitual tongues. Language is ultimately what the religious and the secular have in common—language, that is to say, a yearning for a new way both of wording the world and of worlding language or whatever word is the heart of religion. Everyone that is spoken to is also spoken for and is at home with that for which there is no name, no word—only words.

Dependent as words may be on their etymology, their meaning hangs no less on usage and circumstance and often consists in breaking loose from them. Words branch out and seed into new meanings, at once arbitrary and contingent. Words, Humpty Dumpty would claim, determine their meaning and yet are in turn determined by their use, as every performative utterance would show: we no sooner speak than we are spoken for. "No man is an island." No word is a monad. Words lock up with instead of locking themselves out of one another. They canvass each other, knitting a language that they edit and are edited by, if only because in the end the symbolic function of language must rest on the literal signifiers that make it up. Except perhaps for mathematics, no language is therefore purely descriptive or literal . . . pardon the slip of the pen. I meant: no language is so symbolic as to be merely symbolic, that is, literally symbolic—in which case, neither literal nor symbolic.

Language turns lips into words, flesh into a metaphor of spirit, the human into a condition of the divine, time into a timing of the eternal. Through language, nothing is achieved that is not transformed. Language is a transformer. Lying between the subjective and the objective, between subject and object, it transforms and alters even while embodying our understanding both of the world and of ourselves. Both the self and the world are through one another mirrored in language even as, through language, they mirror one another, and yet language is no mirage, except for Narcissus. Words are ciphers, of which language is the parable, though not in the sense of a story (of what happened) but in that of a scenario—of what is yet to be enacted. Not unlike ducks and drakes on the surface of water, words melt into phrases, through which they sustain the paradox of language: they mean nothing of themselves. Nor would they come to terms with one another were it not for the parabolic role of language in depicting and enacting fictions of the real. We can no more see the real face-to-face than we can face God and not die. Nor can even this be actually stated, except through the parabolic fiction that language itself is. Seeing God face-to-face would amount to turning God into an object of language that would moreover lie outside of language and consist in this or that, in rather what God is than *that* God is. That what God is outside of language is nothing that language can say is precisely what language shows—better still, what language hears. Like a parabolic antenna. The meaning of a word hangs on what it is groping for and lies not so much behind as ahead of the word. Meaning looks forward. Meaning is like bridging gaps between words. It lies agape between words. However anchored in antecedents, such an act of meaning is paradoxically less retrospective than prospective.

A paramount instance of this parabolic instrumentation of language is a key word of this essay, "secular"—a word whose paradoxical impact is to this day felt both through the cultural identification of our spiritual tradition and conversely through the spiritual identification of our cultural tradition. Over the centuries, this impact is of such magnitude that, shedding a new light on the "secular," it affects what is meant by its antonym, "religious" (with which it forms a pair), and, ultimately, by "religion" itself (of which it partakes though without subservience). It is no surprise, then, if the term "secular" stands in need of some preliminary clarification. And no surprise either if, delving into the genealogy of its uses, we find that the same can be said about another key word, the Latin term for which is *mundus* ("world," or *monde* in French and *Welt* in German).

As for "secular," it stems from the noun *saeculum* (also spelled *seculum* or *seclum*), which designates the span of time that lasts for one generation (33 years and 4 months), and is subsequently extended to what we call a century (as is still attested by the French *siècle*). By that time, so to speak, *saeculum* tips over into what is meant by "world" (as in *le siècle de Louis XIV* or *The World of Dinosaurs*), for which Latin already has *mundus*, which is both a noun and an adjective. As a noun, *mundus* means world. It also means universe and serves to render the Greek *cosmos*, with which it moreover shares a cosmetic inclination toward beauty. As an adjective, it means clean, pure. While the verb *mundo* means to clean or purify, another adjective, *mundanus*, qualifies a person as a world citizen. But the idea of cleansing or purification still hangs around. It persists through the French *immonde*, "impure, unclean," with which, oddly enough, the French *monde* has consistently been identified in traditional religious language.

On the other hand, qualified in late antiquity as *aureum* by Tacitus and Virgil, and thus bent into evoking the golden age, *saeculum* designates this world, this life, the present order, the present world (AD 815) by the time Christianity settles down. It branches out into a constellation of cognates, signifiers, and concepts, all of which underline a lexical kinship that, while attesting the initial temporal pointer mentioned earlier, girds it with a spatial dimension. *Saeculum* denotes an experience of the human condition that is all the more temporal for taking on the configuration of a given space. But it *is given* only as is, whether natural or historical, an environment (in both the existential and the ecological sense, and of which *Umwelt* is the German word), which is yet to be *construed* and built or even landscaped into a world, equally ecological and existential (*Welt*).

Worth observing at this point is that, of this landscaping, the semantic topology suggested by *saeculum*'s two key terms owes its lexical instrumentation to Latin. With the exception of "secularism" (1846 according to *The Oxford Universal Dictionary*, 1850 according to *The Oxford Dictionary of the Christian Church*), practically all the terms derived from *saeculum* have shown up and developed during or in the wake of the Latin phase of our cultural phraseology and its rhetoric. *Saecularitas*, attested before

Preface | xiii

1535 (according to the *OUD*), already occurs by 1130, though perhaps it is still afflicted with hangovers from Tertullian's wrongheaded or, more exactly, undiscerning suspicions of pagan worldliness. Let us say it wavers between worldliness and, if not worldhood, at least the status or station in life of most members or institutions of Christendom, including the secular clergy (of a diocese) as distinguished from the regular clergy (of a religious order). This is a distinction that, as we shall see, is adumbrated by *secularizo* (1378), the Latin verb for reducing a priest from the status of regular to secular clergy. But it is a distinction that also anticipates later configurations of this process when, according to F. Lichtenberger, with the treaty of Westphalia (1648, and in English by 1706, according to the *OUD*), "secularization" refers to the transfer of church property or institutions to civil authorities.

Far from being haphazard, this peregrination of meaning even displays an unmistakable Ariadne's thread that takes one back not only to the twin meanings of secular but also to the by-now equally twin meanings of *saeculum* and *mundus*. Enfranchising the worldhood of the world from all religious contempt, this idea of the secular as an inherent dimension of faith could and should have been perceived as the cultural hallmark of the biblical tradition. Otherwise, were the world denied its intrinsic worth, there would be no stage on which the dignity of the human person could be played out. Even before there was a word for it, so to speak, secularity as a dimension of faith was a fact. Our consciousness of it, though the word had not yet happened, had been aroused long before "secularism" was invented. Coined by Holyoake, it was intended to mean what, here, is hopefully conveyed by "secularity." No sooner crafted than hijacked, however, Holyoake's "ideas were later developed into extreme atheism" by C. Bradlaugh, a freethinker and social activist. (S.v. "Secularism," *The Oxford Dictionary of the Christian Church,* ed. F. L. Cross and E. A. Livingstone [London: Oxford University Press, 1974].) In contrast to "secularity," which in a presumably world-denying mentality nevertheless manages to reverse steam and affirm the world, "secularism" is diverted into denying religion and conveying an ideology as fervid as the pseudo-religion it rejects. Had Holyoake's insight been preserved—culturally, not to say theologically, speaking—the secularization of the Judeo-Christian tradition might logically appear by now as one of Christianity's major claims to fame.

Instead, succumbing to a general failure of nerve, Christianity went into conflict with modernity. Isolating and blinding itself, it also turned a deaf ear to the harbingers of a new type of religiosity arising in the wake of the industrial and technological revolutions. It yielded to the temptation of confusing this process of secularization with the marginalization of the Christian establishment begun since the onset of modernity.

Be that as it may, throughout the Middle Ages, the secular is by and large subordinated to the religious, with a significant emblematic exception: of two clergymen of equal rank, the secular has precedence over the regular. Even so, the world makes sense through the church. With the advent of the Reformation, the terms are practically reversed: it is up to the church to make sense through the world. Luther and Calvin carry this out by reconverting priesthood and laity into one another. The so-called priesthood of all believers makes no sense unless the religious and the secular, without being confused, are interchangeable with one another in the discharge of their respective functions, whether spiritual or temporal. Luther appeals to a prince begging him to call a council, and Calvin is expelled from theocratic Geneva—or should I have said anarchic Geneva! This surreptitious linking of anarchy and theocracy is no step taken by inadvertence, either. Unlike the hierarchical dialectic of the sacred and the profane, the critical and self-critical or iconoclastic and prophetic dialectic of the religious and the secular calls for a radical conversion or reconversion of our religious paradigm. Moving from a world-negating to a world-affirming, from a sacral to a utopic, paradigm, religion calls not for changing worlds but for changing this world, the sole arena of a faith that one can live by only once and for all.

Clearly, "secularization" was not invented by modernity, yet to estranged ears secularization is so modern sounding as to stupefy anyone with a mind open enough to learn what it originally means aside from the transfer of a priest from regular to diocesan status. It consists in implementing a privilege of the pope and in reducing the status of a priest to that of a layman, or in the conversion of institutions or functions from ecclesiastical to secular (state or public) authority, to the so-called secular arm. Similarly, ecclesiastical courts, faced with the probability of issuing or enforcing verdicts at odds with or repellent to their dignity as officers of the church, often appealed to "secular courts" and, ironically, laid the bases for "secular" claims to autonomy. This autonomy is largely achieved by the time of the Treaty of Westphalia when Protestant princes of Germany expropriated church establishments. Followed in this respect by the French Revolution and Napoleon, they were long preceded by the emperor Henry

II of Germany, not to mention all those earlier leaders of the Frankish Empire that indulged in church expropriations.

But is "expropriation" still the right term? Like hospitals and universities in the United States, many others elsewhere in the world have been disconnected from their ecclesiastical affiliation. The Pauluskirche in Frankfurt and the Fontevrault Abbey in France have, like many others, been turned into cultural centers. Rather than expropriated, they have been "converted" from one use or function to another, not necessarily at odds with one another. A Christian shoemaker does not make Christian shoes. He sees to it that the shoes are well made and that the poor are shod. There need be no hostility and no exclusiveness between the secular or temporal and the religious or spiritual any more than there is between the so-called religious or regular clergy and the secular clergy, whether they belong to a religious order and its rule or to a diocese.

The cross-fertilization of *mundus* (world, *Welt*, *monde*) and *saeculum* (this present age, this world) is so staggering that, from cacophony into symphony, it seems to stretch language beyond some kind of sound barrier: "world without end" simply renders *in saecula saeculorum*, and, as the eternal breaks into or invests time, *saeculum* turns into a *kairos*, an opportunity, an occasion for timing a worlding of the word become flesh. I cannot accordingly resist considering worldhood and secularity as isomorphous terms. In German, *weltlich* and *Weltlichkeit*, derived from *Welt* (world), simply render secular and secularity. We get a hint of this comforting, though at times disconcerting, amphibological use of terms with Paul Tillich, as I have tried to show elsewhere. This can especially be felt when, switching from German to English, he has to cope with the questionable and philologically hybrid American conundrum of "the sacred and the secular," a coupling against nature yet so widespread in the middle of the last century. No wonder religion was caught in a vice: it could not tell which end was up.

Even supposing it has somewhat come to its senses by now, to the detriment of the more biblical prophetic stance, religion has practically been engulfed by the general obsession with the sacred. It is as if, in the waning stages of modernity, its trompe-l'oeil bulwarks, rationalism and scientism (no surrogates of the secular), had finally come to rest in the lap of the sacred, making up for the demise of God. A cheap substitute for the holiness of God, for the God who is never said to be sacred but holy, and surviving an obsolescent Christianity, the sacred once again stands for the acme and most subtle form of self-crowning achievement in the religious pretension of the primacy of antiquity over the new, of the past over the future.

Even Tertullian (d. 240), with his identification of the *saeculum* with pagan worldliness (*De pudicitia* 1; *De Anima* 46), looked forward and somehow paved the way for his third-century contemporary Cyprian and successors like Saint Jerome (331–420) or Saint Augustine (354–430) with whom *saeculum* or its derivatives designate the present order by contrast with "religio," the ecclesiastical order. Though a fragrance of worldliness may surround such use of the term (as it still does with Karl Barth), a step was nevertheless being taken that will become a giant one when, with—or for that matter, in spite of—modernity and its aftermath, we move from the world as objective to the world as subjective reality and from being to language as the prism through which yearns to be grasped a self that would lack nothing if, *verbum caro* (like the word become flesh), it only could lack itself.

Finally, quite appropriate in this connection, is the notion of "adiaphoricity." The term stems from the Greek noun *adiaphoron,* a thing of itself indifferent as to its use and meaning. From Melanchthon to Friedrich Schleiermacher, it refers to matters of indifference with respect to faith and its obligations—matters (like theater) that, adding pleasure to life, could and, Schleiermacher adds, even should be indulged, thus marking the passage from worldliness to worldhood.

Acknowledgments

This book was anticipated by various lectures and publications, for which I shall remain beholden to my hosts. To these generous hosts, academic peers or editors and publishers, I wish to record here my gratitude for permission to excerpt from or incorporate materials made public under their moral authority and listed as follows:

"Democracy, Solidarity, Utopia: A Theological Approach" (Richard Rorty on Ethics and Politics), Centre de Recherches Interdisciplinaires en Bioéthique, U.L.B., Brussels 1993, published as "Démocratie, solidarité, utopie," in *Richard Rorty, ambiguïtés et limites du postmodernisme*, ed. G. Hottois and M. Weyembergh (© Librairie Philosophique J. Vrin, Paris, 1994; http://www.vrin.fr), and "Democratie, solidariteit, utopie," in *Richard Rorty, ironie, politiek en postmodernisme*, ed. G. Hottois, M. van den Bossche, and M. Weyembergh (Antwerpen-Baarn: Hadewijk, 1994).

"Anarchy and Holiness," *The Ellul Forum* 13 (1994): 11–13.

"Ethics, Theology, and the Postmodern Mind," University of South Florida, Tampa, April 11, 1995.

"The Death of God: From the Story of God to God as Scenario," University of South Florida, Tampa, April 13, 1995.

"Eloge du séculier," Université des Sciences Humaines, Strasbourg, spring 1995; "In Praise of the Secular: The Biblical Roots of the Post-Modern," Syracuse University, October 26, 1995, and Montclair State University, October 30, 1995.

"Pluralism and the Secular," Montclair State University, October 30, 1995.

"The Denatured Nature of Ethics: In Praise of the Secular," in *Philosophie de la religion entre éthique et ontologie*, ed. Marco M. Olivetti (Padua: Cedam/Biblioteca dell' Archivio di Filosofia, 1996).

"L'autre et le temps," *Autres Temps* 57 (1998): 47–59; published, thanks to an initial translation from French by Warren Clarnette of Australia, as "The Otherness of Time," *Journal for Cultural and Religious Theory* 1 (1999): 1; www.jcrt/Journal.

"Theology and the Secular," American Academy of Religion Annual Meeting, Nashville, November 19, 2000, subsequently rewritten for *Secular Theology: American Radical Theological Thought*, ed. Clayton Crockett (London: Routledge, 2001).

"Technology, Theology, and the Secular," a series of lectures organized in the fall of 2000 by Nam-Gung Chan, delivered at various academic and theological institutions of Korea, and summarized in Kim Young Seon, ed., *Sae si dae, sae sin hak/New Age, New Theology* (Seoul: Hyupseong sinhak yeon ku non tsong 5, Hyupsung seo. Kyo huoe, sinhak yeonguso, Ki dok kyo das han kamri hyoe hang bo tsulpan kuk, 2001).

The lines from "yours is the music for no instrument," copyright 1923, 1951, © 1991 by the Trustees for the E. E. Cummings Trust, copyright © 1976 by George James Firmage, from COMPLETE POEMS: 1904–1962 by E. E. Cummings, edited by George J. Firmage, are used by permission of Liveright Publishing Corporation.

Gratefully indebted for the above to all those whose names I have mentioned, I am all the more pleased to thank also James B. Wiggins, Michael S. Kogan, Darrell Fasching, and Yang Myung-Su. More especially, however, I must give thanks to Cathie Brettschneider for her exceptional talent in debunking my idiosyncrasies and for her stewardship in facilitating the flow of my argument. For the generous and no less critical suggestions of readers at once clement and rigorous in their expectations, I wish to thank an anonymous reader for the Press and, in particular, to acknowledge my debt to Edith Wyschogrod for the most pertinent advice I received in so shaping this text as to render it even more hospitable to the reader.

Unless otherwise stated, all translations into English are my own.

Praise of the Secular

Introduction

Religious and secular: these are terms that through the centuries used to form a pair. They were not confused with one another. Nor were they ever dissociated and disjoined from each other. Through the ages of faith, even while apparently the secular was subordinated to the religious and the world like the body was held in contempt, they conditioned one another. And they did so from those days on, all the way to the time when, as was contended, the religious itself, if it must be grasped by its despisers, had to be construed in terms of the secular. But throughout, the religious only *showed the way to* the secular—in either sense of this phrase. In any case, an all the more precarious equilibrium was somehow maintained.

Put into question by the growing discord between science and faith, this equilibrium was further strained when, seriously overwhelmed, science gave way to scientism and religion to fideism. But neither could really go it alone. Reason itself had to be chastened, and it was. So also was religion: it had to come to grips with its own failure of nerve. And that is precisely what, willy-nilly, religion is doing when it shifts from one paradigm to another, from the contrast of beings with being-itself as meaning-giving center of the world order to language as milieu of any world order; this shift accounts for the fact that now it is the secular that shows the way to the religious. Which of them shows the way to the other is but a matter of strategy, not of preeminence. Even with the promulgation of the Law, God actually is already brought down to earth. As the Maker, God makes all things new, but nothing is per se divine. Through the word become flesh, the religious is likewise inscribed in the secular.

The religious is not today threatened by the secular any more than it was in the past. Nor is faith threatened by science or by the rational. Though they both need logic, neither science nor faith is exclusively dependent on it. Even while at their service, ultimately logic always defeats itself. Therefore any would-be victory of faith over science or of science over faith is only Pyrrhic. Likewise of theism over atheism, and of atheism over theism. God, and for the same reason faith, has no other milieu than language. The same holds true for science when it is faced with the intrinsic meaninglessness of facts and, even more drastically, of the world.

Atheism, especially from a biblical perspective, was never a threat to "God." Idolatry, yes. Because the idol, far from being no God, both is and is not God.[1] It is an idol and it is not. Though we worship it, we can do so only by mistaking it for God. We forget not only that, from a biblical standpoint, such a God is no God but also, conversely, that no God is God—not so much because God is beyond God as because no God is beyond language. And because of language, we can no sooner worship God than we turn God into an idol—into a God's-eye view of our own in the light of which, obviously, God can be God only for *us*, not for *them*. We end up crediting the notion that language is of an altogether different ilk for the believer and the unbeliever. This is a conundrum that would resolve itself were it not for the extralinguistic contention of such a cleavage. Believer and unbeliever can be separated only by what they have in common—a language, unless and until it has been frozen by either or both of them. Once frozen, it will feed their respective ideologies and in turn be fed on, by fundamentalism in one case and by secularism in the other, the former begging for the mantle of a fideism it further disfigures, the latter arrogating to itself leftovers from an incoherent scientism.

Still, for all their mutual antagonism, both fundamentalism and secularism have, at least so far as Western culture is concerned, been equally weaned on the same intellectual as well as spiritual tradition. It is a tradition that stems no less from Athens than from Jerusalem. It partakes of their respective utopic vision, whether of a world that God so loves as to make all things new or of a world that lies west of the world, from the eastern to the western shores of the Mediterranean and through the Atlantic to the Far West and the Pacific rim of the Far East.

Yet on the threshold of a new millennium, both fundamentalism and secularism equally mar the horizon of Western culture and its progressive surrender to a more global approach. In spite of the tradition to which their roots can be traced, each in its own way rests on the fatal cleavage of the religious and the secular, a cleavage ideologically beclouded and benumbed by contentions of a radical but equally dogmatic opposition not so much between faith and science as between their surrogates. Hence each overlooks the fact that religion is not reducible to fundamentalism or that the secular is by no means the exclusive hunting ground of secularism.

I have just described the overall framework of this book, in keeping with which the various cognate themes of each chapter are elaborated: (1) theology or, for that matter, faith as vindication of the secular and the growing substitution of a world to be hallowed for a world to be held in contempt; (2) the secular as horizon of the incarnation and the word become flesh as worlding of the word in view of a utopic or eschatic (rather than merely soteriological) understanding of the kingdom of God; this implies that (3) whatever morality is achieved, through deeds of custom and habit inherited from the past, cannot be transmitted unless its accumulated wisdom of the past makes room for an ethic of the unprecedented; and (4) that the secular was an eminently religious category long before it became itself a secular category is further clarified by examining the contributions of Paul Tillich, Jacques Ellul, and Richard Rorty; I then conclude this chapter with remarks that will provide the transition gradually both to (5) a reappraisal of the two bodies of the Christ (religious and secular) in the light of a technologically globalized and yet rootless culture and to (6) the secular theme par excellence—namely, the worlding of the word or explicitation of the incarnation in relation to time, to that which having, like religion, no past has no future, either. It happens once and for all, *in saecula saeculorum* (i.e., for ever), according to the classical language of religion and its implicit contention that language—rather than nature or history—is the "milieu" of the human as it is that of the divine. Likewise, it is the milieu of both the religious and the secular and their respective synonyms in the light of which, if life is at all worth living, it is worth living once and for all.

The first chapter thus begins by recalling that, however condescendingly, the secular, because it was never actually severed from the religious, formed a collaborating pair with the religious, as did natural and supernatural, and immanence and transcendence or temporal and eternal. Whether subordinated to the religious during the Middle Ages, or posed as the horizon of the religious with the advent of the Reformation, the secular has always been one side and the religious the other side of one and the same coin. Faith, understood either ontologically (i.e., in terms of a life predicated on changing worlds after death) or eschatologically (i.e., in terms of a life predicated on changing the world here and now), is what they had in common. It was and still is today their common denominator.

Whatever else is meant by faith, it is what confronts the human being with the task of being human. Being human is no matter of mere biology or of physiology so much as of language: in being human, the human being not only is a speaking animal but also is spoken for. Language is the medium, the "milieu" for a human being in the process of being human. For being human, though all too human, is yet the very condition of "God" as word, gathered to no more than a mere word in the dictionary. Words are not found in nature. Nor is what they describe found in nature. Much less is God found in nature. God lies in language even to the extent of belying or of being belied by it. Either way, this is for a good reason: the realm of language is eminently cultural rather than natural, and therefore it displays a twofold dimension, religious and secular, from whose polarities and tensions, it must be noted, the polarity and tension of nature and the spirit is never absent. Nor is any other kind of polarity and tension absent.

Yet "secular" has become the ugly duckling of Western culture. Apparently denied the least inkling of nobility, it stands in relation to the religious as did a vassal to the suzerain whose protection it obliges. It is only when the secular is pried loose that, giving illegitimate birth to so-called secularism (1846), it is turned into an ideological shibboleth of defiance against every conditioning of life that smacks of religion. Even so, alternately, the secular is at other times perceived more positively. Thus standing rather in keeping with the adiaphoricity of the world as arena of faith, it pervades the whole gamut of a world come of age (Bonhoeffer); but at best it is looked upon as a prodigal son, secretly envied more than held in contempt by his brother. But then because the secular ultimately challenges *every* preconception of one's commitment to being human, it is, at worst, perceived as a threat to the religious tradition.

The secular is neither a threat nor an antidote. It must recover the prestige to which it is entitled, even as the world does when *nomos* or *torah* (law) takes over from *physis* (nature) and the secular, not unlike nature, is fulfilled by grace rather than destroyed. In a global culture in which faith is no longer determined by geography, the secular rather than religion is what we all have in common.

The second chapter pursues this argument in the light of the incarnation, the story of which in the prologue of John's Gospel reads like a creation story. God speaks and the thing happens. The word is worlded. God so loves the world that he gives his only Son. The word becomes flesh. And the word is worlded even as it is embodied. The cosmological and the existential are not fused but belong together, as do the spatial and the temporal or, for that matter, male and female. Some—possibly shying away from calling a spade a spade—even speak of the incarnation as an "intemporation." But because they would extend such intemporation to no outright secularizing of the word, they confine it to some breaking of the eternal into the temporal or of the eschatological into the historical. Although muzzled, the message could still be heard: with or without the church and its institutions, the kingdom is at hand even while the word is being worlded unless and until the times are fulfilled. And when the times are fulfilled, the religious and saving word itself is heard ringing loud and clear through this very worlding of the word: there is no temple in the New Jerusalem. The secular has come into its own.

The reality of God is at stake in and through the reality of this world. And because this world is a world in which the very self of God is brought into question, the utopianism of the kingdom of God is kept from being swallowed by any overpowering, though human, all-too-human, ideology of salvation. God need not die in order for us to be. Nor do we, human beings, need to spend our lives yearning for a world beyond this world. Faith is not aimed at changing worlds but at changing the world by letting the word be worlded.

Unlike Jesus, who dies taking God at God's word, we think that God is too divine for words and that it is not enough for Jesus to die; he must die as does a God that dies and is born again. We make a God of him who—unlike a Jew standing for the man that does not take himself for God—stands for the Jew who, because he is freed from bondage as though he were raised from the dead, cannot ever take himself for God, unless he should turn God into an idol, a private God.

Through the word become flesh, through Jesus as the Christ, God "falls" in the public domain: we are "stuck" with Jesus—and need not be, had we not hastened to take him for a God. Forgetting that God is no God that only dies to be born again, we turn the utopic theme of the worlding of the word into an ideology of salvation in an afterlife, as though this life were not worth living here and now, once and for all.

Calling for the worlding of the word, the incarnation also calls for an embodiment of the word, giving mouth to a body by turning lips into words. It belies the subsequent tendency of a church so engrossed with salvation in an afterlife that, unwittingly, in spite of Paul's insistence on the body of Christ as both personal and collective embodiment of the faithful, it will obstinately unleash waves upon waves of contempt for the world as well as for the body. The present upsurge of concern with the secular—and the body—can only remind it that God dwells, not on this or that mountain, not in this or that church, but in language, and that language consists in both debunking and yearning for God. It is both iconic and iconoclastic, religious and secular. This amounts to saying that, through language, faith is no monopoly of the religious. It is what the religious and the secular have in common.

The third chapter tries to show that, in contrast to natural or so-called historical phenomena, the religious is a fiction of language—call it a myth, if you will. So is the secular. Neither one, in view of the human being's confrontation with the call to being human, is an option except in and through language, an inscription of time into space and of space into time and, by the same token, of the religious in the secular and of the secular in the religious. To wit: church bells, thanks to which a Western landscape *rings* differently from an Eastern landscape. How different? That is the question, since the difference is no matter of abstract time or of stubborn space so much as of timing and spacing of language. It is a language that, however geographically circumscribed and determined, is universal, albeit proleptically, so long as it yearns for the God it keeps on debunking, or because, having a word for God, it ultimately refrains from taking God for granted. Language leads to no God that it can take for granted—for the same reason it is allergic to the idol. It is likewise neither theonomous nor heteronomous.

Indeed, just because language does not take God for granted, it is autonomous. Otherwise, there would be a language for believers and another for unbelievers, a dichotomy it cannot tolerate without sacralizing itself. So far as the biblical tradition is concerned, such a language would stand in flagrant contradiction to the rhetoric of both the Ten Commandments and the incarnation. It would stand in contradiction both to the logic of worlding the word and to that of its concomitant process of hallowing the world. This is another way of saying that both law and gospel hang on that radical otherness of God that is here assessed, not in terms of the sacred, but in terms of the holy in whose light the world is all that is the case only because, being unprecedented, it is kept from alienating itself, whether by reason of God or of no God. This is so because nothing happens except through language. And because whatever happens through language happens once and for all, language encompasses all that is, even nothing more than all that is; it has an autonomy of its own in whose light alone God is holy and, rather than either present (theism) or absent (atheism), is radically other. Because language is thus essentially theological, it can both exceed and fall short of God.

Language shies away from any God's-eye view. To wit: the biblical notion of creation or, for that matter, of incarnation, not to mention the law whose implementation through the commandments both exceeds and falls short of God (as Jesus points out in the parable of the Last Judgment). No one lives up to it who does not live it up once and for all. God is not without the world, but the world is not God. God is life, but life is not divine. Especially in the christic view, there is no God of which life and this world could be the exclusive representation. Likewise, there is no creation but *ex nihilo* (that is, unprecedented). Or else God would be an idol that only lords it over its creation, and nothing could happen that was not fated.

No time comes before time. Nothing happens that is not unprecedented. Unlike history, natural or otherwise, time does not repeat itself. What happens is only that which happens once and for all—*sub specie aeternitatis* (in the light of eternity), in the light of language rather than nature as realm of creation, or again of language rather than history as realm of the (eternal) word become flesh; that is, broadly translated, once and for all if only in terms of an ethic, call it of language or of faith, that consists in changing the world rather than changing worlds, of this world as arena of faith rather than as object of its contempt.

In the fourth chapter, going through the positions put forth by Tillich, Ellul, and Rorty, I try to show that because of its vindication of the secular, religion, having long since turned into an obsession with salvation, must finally come to grips with the mandates of its charter. It must switch (back) to the recovery of the utopic streak of its grammar and rhetoric.

This is a streak that, from Homer and Abraham on, by way of Plato or even Aristotle and the prophets, to Jesus, who proclaims the kingdom rather than salvation, has persistently been characteristic of the Western frame of mind. The Greeks have always "gone West." And though perhaps in contrast to Israel and because of Rome's geographical situation, Paul (who could have gone East as had many, Jewish or not, before him)—even Paul—wants to "go West." More significantly, moving westward instead of disavowing Judaism, Paul manages to deregulate it. He descralizes Jerusalem. Rehearsing nothing but the Old Testament, for the dialectic of Israel and the nations he substitutes the dialectic of the holy and the secular. This he sums up in the image of the body, personal or collective, as the temple of God (or of the Spirit), as the body of Christ in which there is neither Greek nor Jew, neither male nor female, and (depending on what is meant by these terms I make bold of adding) neither God nor the human. In a subtle move, Paul even points out that the world, the secular—unlike the religious?—is full of gods. It should be rid of them and, through the victory of faith, recover its worldhood (the German for which, *Weltlichkeit*, primarily means secularity). Paul's is an autonomous, iconoclastic, christic vision of life together.

Teasingly though not arbitrarily, the fifth chapter focuses on the two bodies of the Christ (mystical and political, Jewish and Greek, personal and collective, religious and secular). Under the guise of this twofold body of the Christ, my aim is to show that the historically predominant sacral understanding of faith as a social phenomenon (with its hierarchical as well as exclusivistic gravity) is no longer operative. It must give way to a utopic overhaul that harks back to the Greek legacy and is equally rooted in the biblical tradition as embedded in the prophets' heritage.

Given idiosyncratic circumstances as well as possibly ideolectic constraints, the christic vision of life together that stemmed from this heritage was subsequently adapted to the prevailing mood of the times. It lost some of its punch and was thwarted, or at least somewhat muted. It was not discarded. But this is not the place for a demonstration of that.

We have been shifting from one religious paradigm to another. We are in the process of switching from a mythologically to a technologically oriented paradigm of religion, from the symbols of a sacral understanding of nature to those of a utopic vision of existence. (I dwell on their opposition only for the sake of convenience. Technology is as old as the human being's first attempt at being human, and myth deals no less with meaning than it does with saying or telling.) Between them, some might argue that what has been taking place is a denaturing of religion (Tillich). The world has been disenchanted. Others would instead contend that, disenchanted with the world it has bequeathed us, religion itself has grown all the more disenchanting and needs to be overhauled. Given its traditional affinities with technology and the spirit of utopia (Garden of Eden, Promised Land, kingdom of God, body of Christ, New Jerusalem, etc.), it has all the skills needed to retool its language. And such is this language that it has always consisted in bridging the unbridgeable, the divine and the human, Greek and Jew, human being and being human, as well as beginning and end, already and not yet, this world and the next.

In other words, religion is today not so much denatured as it is suffering from something like mental fatigue. It is not so much threatened by the secular as it has slackened in its ability to rebound and adapt to the situation. Understandably. In the planetary village, which has replaced the traditional parish and its territorial connotations, religion must, on top of the bargain, yet cope with its own deregulation among other types of deregulation. It must cope with its own timing.

Timing the eternal is the theme of the sixth and concluding chapter. But then the question is not whether existence comes before or after essence. It unfolds and is folded upon itself, and the question is whether I am up to par with its timing. Being is timing. Rather than a matter of genealogy, timing is a matter of hoped-for and unexpected faith. Even as essential and existential, because they are mutually congruous, hinge on one another, so do eternal and temporal or everlasting and ephemeral. After all, is there anything that, lasting a day, did not "actually" last an eternity? Or anything that, momentous, lasting for ever, did not last once and for all, however brief its moment? As the book of Proverbs (12:19) puts it, "Truthful lips endure for ever, but a lying tongue is but for a moment." Centuries later, even for Kierkegaard, no moment is as unpremeditated as the instant. And nothing is more instantaneous than that which happens once and for all and, worlding the word, is an instance of the eternal; as Latin would have it, it lies *in saecula saeculorum*.

The temporal, like the word become flesh, is what happens in time and on time. And ever since the creation, whatever happens in and on time is a world come of age, so secular as not to belie the worlding of the word with which it is coextensive. So secular as to provide religion with an occasion, a *kairos*, for rehearsing itself and enchanting the world—a world without which it can only sink in either of its twin foes, secularism or fundamentalism.

Theology and the Secular

For it was not through law that Abraham, or his posterity, was given the promise that the world should be his inheritance, but through the righteousness that came from faith.

—Romans 4:13

If a man merely stares at the world, while another not only sees but questions it, the world does not appear differently to them; but appearing the same to both, it is dumb to one and answers the other. Or rather it speaks to all, but only those understand it that compare its answer with the truth that is within them.

—Saint Augustine, *Confessions*

Nothing is secularized that was not religious. Though the secular has been expurgated from theological discourse and divested of any congruence with the religious dimension of the basic experience of life, it rightfully belongs to the sphere of faith. Hanging on the retrieval of the lost pertinence of the secular and its import is the very relevance of the ethic of faith to the religious pluralism of today's shrinking world.

"Secular"—no other word has been so pried loose of its semantic context. Suspected of fostering the so-called death of God, it has been both acclaimed and vilified. This is possibly because what brings the secular into play—and, as expected, causes an inflation of the secular—deals with the growing, nagging, and contagious conviction that no sooner is God worshipped than even God becomes an idol. Concretely put, the secular is brought into play when religion, never prone to resist its own sacralization, tips into the ideological framework of a preconceived belief system, while culture is cut loose from its meaning-giving center and is left stranded in the "no-man's-land" of a superfluous God. Instead of coming to grips with culture, religion settles down, as would a fossil amid equally superannuated artifacts. The ideological edge of the classic notion of the God that dies in order to be born again gives way to the death of God as a cultural phenomenon calling for an even more radical revolution than ever achieved by any religious reformation.

The death of God thus heralds no victory of the secular over the religious. Nor does it consist in the reversal of their roles. It raises a sudden question against a double albeit legitimate pretension: on the one hand, against religion and its pretension to cultural appetence, and on the other, against culture and its pretension to religious appetence. Once religion is fossilized, culture is betrayed, preyed on, and plundered by the sacred, whatever the pretext, whether a quest for identity or the treacherous comfort of communitarian bonds. The less God is credible, the more credible the sacred is. With the death of God, the necessary correlation of religion and culture no longer hinges on the equilibrium so far achieved between the religious—or, in biblical terms, the holy (not to be confused with the sacred)—and the secular (not to be confused with the profane). In contrast to the dialectic of the sacred and the profane, which takes God or any surrogate of God for granted, the dialectic of the holy (or the religious) and the secular never takes God for granted, unless God were turned into an idol.[1]

Never meant to drive a wedge between God and the world, much less to drive God out of the world by first insinuating and then widening a gap between them, "secular" has become the unwilling and all-the-more-maligned carrier of their falling-out. Often put forth, in religious circles, as if to conjure some would-be metatastic evolution of this falling-out and yet more or less contrived as its syndrome, the secular owes its rise less to the yawning gap between religion and culture than to the self-inflicted demise of Christianity. It calls for a new religious paradigm.

Religion as Vindication of the Secular

As already suggested, "secular" actually was only the antonym of "religious," not its Manichaean opposite, or its negation: they formed a pair, never to be cleaved one from the other. Together, they belonged to one and the same worldview and belonged with one another (as implied in the twin notions of regular and secular clergy). No sooner are they split from one another than each seems to come apart at the seams. "Secular" becomes a shibboleth for a newfangled ideology of liberation from the past.

Or else it is looked upon as an orphan or a kind of prodigal son that is in the process of squandering his father's religious inheritance: ours is a culture that wants both to erase everything and to forget nothing. Above all, it must no longer be denied the courage to break through the positivism of a situation that feeds on the assumption that religion is a thing of the past—to be sure, an allegation yet to be proven entirely groundless. Given many a traditional definition, religion has largely dealt with memorizing the past, even keeping it alive medically through artificial means if necessary. It has often overlooked the fact that, by itself, it consists in only one side of the coin of which the other is the secular: they belong together. Or the fact that just as blood runs through both arteries and veins, so does life—faith, too—run through the religious and the secular. Remove the heart, or kill God, and the same finger is pointing at us: we have also killed the secular or turned it into the paroxysmal parody of an obsolescent religion.

No other word has been more maligned than the word "secular." Its connotations encompass so diverse a debauchery of meaning as to throw into a dizzying puzzle of bewilderment anyone who is endowed with the least love of language as sole bearer of religion. These connotations run the whole gamut from antonym of "religious" to synonym of "atheist." Words are weaned on other words. Like Russian dolls, they achieve a meaning by shedding another; they grow into meanings by which they are outgrown, regardless of their etymological roots, or because of them.

Even so, "secular" is a word whose fate has been worse even than that of the word "God." Because "God" would name that which has no name, it is but a noun and, ultimately, not so much a proper noun as one that is common to all that is. It belongs no more to the religious than it belongs to the secular. That, for supposedly being extruded from the realm of daily concerns, God alone can and must be eschewed by the secular is no less an erroneous contention than the corresponding allegation that, for positing God only by intruding God into the kernel of memory, religion identifies itself with memory and turns into a survival kit. But the secular is of itself no more future oriented than the religious is past oriented.

Despite preconceived notions, what actually threatens the secular is not the past but the future. What threatens the religious is not the future but the past. From time immemorial, not unlike the albatross burdened by its wings, religion has been weighed down by this fear of having no future. Memory hoarding itself, religion has been oblivious of the fact that, for a religion, the future consists precisely in not having any. Indeed, had religion shed itself of such a fear, it would have kept with the biblical tradition, which holds precisely that true religion has no future and none certainly beyond this world—the *saeculum*. There is no religion in the New Jerusalem or in Jesus's parable of the Last Judgment. Nor is there any in Thomas More's *Utopia*. None either in the world come of age celebrated by Bonhoeffer, though Bonhoeffer himself continued to be caught in the throes of a residual Lutheran dualism and, despite Luther, the condescending look cast upon the world, upon the secular.

Nonetheless, in the contest or mutual testing of the religious and the secular, it is always the religious that is in constant need of "pruning." Likewise, growing as it were together with the religious, the secular ineluctably outgrows religion. Seemingly outdating the traditional compact of religion with culture, the secular still looms on the incompressible horizon of their common commitment to a new world and fades into hope, garnering the expectation of a religion loosened from the memory of fossilized patterns of thinking and believing. To wit, Israel: instead of merely remembering the past, it listens to that God that would be no God should God not make room for the world and should there be no world here and now, should there not be once and for all a world as ephemeral and contingent as it is secular (i.e., a pro-vision of the new heaven and the new earth, of the newness of the world—its worldhood).

The secular is not merely secular. Nothing is secular that is not at the same time symmetrical with something religious. Just that is the paramount reason why traditional theology "must address its own irrelevance."[2] It must consent to the agonizing reappraisal of its own discourse. Theological discourse must recover its credibility in a world come of age ("secularized," as others are wont to say, giving that term a negative inflection meant to drown all positivity to which its pristine meaning is intrinsically entitled).

We talk of the secular much as we do of religion. Used to presuming there is an essence of religion, more immutable than not, we likewise tend to think of the secular as though it too must have an essence. And, of course, that essence should both set it at the opposite end of the spectrum from religion and keep it from shying away from the least pretense of an incontrovertibly self-adjudicated status at the apex of an equally self-programming ideology.

Unfortunately, under the guise of "secularism" such an essence is no sooner identified than its true nature becomes manifest. It festers the secular, just as its counterpart, fundamentalism, festers religion. Worse still, however antagonistic their respective claims may be, fundamentalism and secularism similarly result from an equally positivistic coercion of one prong of the dialectic of the religious and the secular into subservience to the other. Faking each other, they are interchangeable. Not being real twins, they are not self-limiting, either, and they counterfeit or blur and pervert the respective realms of the absolute and the relative, of the transcendent and the immanent. Either by absolutizing the relative (fundamentalism) or by relativizing the absolute (secularism), they disfigure the intrinsic autonomy whether of the religious or of the secular.

Either way, a process is inaugurated that consists in reducing language to some kind of newspeak, so terrorized that it will carry any ideology. In fact, from East to West, this is the age neither of secularism nor of fundamentalism but of each joyfully blending with the other. Not that, here and there, people live in some Dark Age whereas others do not. Ironically, this is an age when no religion can claim to be the best or the only religion. Every religion is the whole religion. Yet they all shy away from embracing the only thing they have in common: not religion (which is why they are divided) but the secular. It is what all the religions have in common. Not unlike the unconscious in Lacan's view, the secular is construed as a language, through whose instrumentality it eventually meshes with the religious and its language. Language is also what the religious and the secular have in common. Or else language would not be iconoclastic, which it must be if the religious is iconoclastic of the secular and the secular is iconoclastic of the religious.

In this light, neither secularism nor fundamentalism can claim to be viable projects. They do, however, provide sociology, or a sociologically attuned mind-set such as ours has become, with enough fuel to keep it sliding down the slippery slope at the bottom of which not only the religious but also the secular lose their respective identities. They are melted in a process that, neither fish nor fowl, is no less abusively called secularization and has less to do with any drive toward the secular—as vested in and vindicated by true religion in keeping with biblical faith—than it has to do with the *dis-habilitation* of religion or the obsolescence of Christianity. Disheveled, bruised, maimed, kidnapped, or raped by would-be specialists more concerned with their own press than with pressing the real issue in the aftermath of the death of God, secularization needs to be salvaged and retrieved. It must recover the meaning of its pristine thrust as one prong of a dialectic of which, in the biblical tradition, the other is perceived as hallowing (or sanctification).

Saying these are theological terms nowadays deprived of their down-to-earth signification is hardly questionable. What is questionable, oddly if ironically enough, are the reasons—in the very sense in which Archibald MacLeish's Job declares in *J.B.* that "God is reasons"—for which the effects of the interface between sanctification (hallowing) and secularization have deserted the mindscape of the imagination even among the American people, whose cultural heritage would no doubt sink into oblivion if Thanksgiving should perchance cease from being emblematic of its spirit.

Yet whether Thanksgiving is a religious or a secular holiday makes no difference. And it makes no difference precisely because of the phenomenological principle at work in the inescapably mutual compatibility between church and world, which held that *ecclesia in mundo latet* (the church is latent in the world) while *mundus in ecclesia patet* (the world is patent in the church), or as Tillich will say, that religion is the substance of culture and culture the form of religion.[3] Precisely because religion means the overcoming of religion (Buber) and its secularization, religion can be overcome only by religion. Correspondingly, secularization can refer to the gradual dismissal of religion only by adepts of some sociology of religion already sentenced to extinguish itself. Like Pinocchio's nose: should it keep growing, there would soon be no Pinocchio left to tell a lie. But of course sociologists who have to make a living will doubtless find, then, another half-truth and switch from one fundamentalism to another, from one secularism to another, prone as some of them are to mistake the sign for what it points to.

Hallowing (or sanctification) and secularization are, on the contrary, the cutting edge of a process through which by "world" is designated not so much a datum as a mandate, not a fate but a destiny, not only the realm of *anankē* (necessity) but also that of *nomos* (i.e., of the possible though it may seem impossible). Thus by "world" is ultimately designated the realm of *logos,* the empowering of the will unable by itself even to do the good that possibly is within its reach, inasmuch as the will precedes everything except itself.⁴ No world comes of age except through the word, as illustrated according to the biblical tradition of creation and incarnation and the fullness of time. Nor does any of these notions entail the least contempt for the world, but they require its defatalization; they entail no disparagement of nature, though they require its desacralization.

In other words, biblical religion does not respond to an order of things enshrined by the dualism of the sacred and the profane. It consists in a dialectic approach of a totally different order, that of the holy and the secular, or, in terms more consonant with the biblical outlook on the world, of the holy and the not-yet holy.⁵ Nothing is more religious than the secular, but then nothing is more secular than the religious, either. One might even go the further step of identifying this approach as a dialectic of the secular and the not-yet secular. It bears repeating: the religious or holy and the secular belong together.⁶

They belong together and, arguably, so do perhaps the sacred and the profane. But in contrast to the prophetic and charismatic aspect of the former, one has to deal with the hierarchical character of the latter. Take Mircea Eliade's well-known definition. Its laconic brevity is more telling than any disquisition that would only burden the evidence. The sacred, says Eliade, is that which is not profane and the profane is that which is not sacred. Standing between them is something like an altar rail. Each is confined within itself rather than to the other, but neither is really self-limiting. Things are the way they are by reason of *anankē* or *physis*. Greek is set above barbarian, Jew above goy. They evince a statically structured order, quite in contrast to the dynamic configuration achieved by the religious and the secular, where the "altar rail" of the sacred and profane lingers on until it is erased from the symbolic imagination by the iconoclastic move toward the priesthood of all believers.

Ordered to one another, the religious and the secular limit themselves. They are self-limiting insofar as each consists, not in secluding itself from or being secluded by the other, but in making room for the other.⁷ The Israelites are expected to make room for the stranger that is within their gates, all the more "naturally" since, unlike Athenians of old, the Israelites form a people by virtue not of their origin but of their calling. Whatever their identity or morality, they can only catch a glimpse of it, not in the mirror of nature, nor in that of history, but in the iconoclastic mirror of the word. Identity does not result from natural sedimentation or from historical sedentarization but in spite of them: it lies in the future, in that which is yet in need of coming to pass. Morality is not a matter of conformity with natural necessity or with historical convention but of eschatological pro-vision. Receiving a stranger may be a show of human morality. It is above all an eschatological act—the identification of oneself, not with but through the other and, likewise, of the chosen people through the nations, of the religious through the secular.

Ultimately, or in biblical terms eschatologically speaking, what counts is what Israel and the nations have in common. And in view of the parable of the Last Judgment and Paul's understanding of the body of Christ, what they have in common comes about only where there is neither Jew nor Greek, neither master nor slave, neither man nor woman, but one world as worlding of the word become flesh.[8] It comes about wherever faith is not the monopoly of religion, and this world is the only world in which one may live by faith—that is, eschatically.

Remember: the Greek word from which *eschatic* is derived refers to that *last* thing or event, by whatever name it is identified, in the light of which all that is at stake in this life stands revealed and "justified" and is at all events in need of that grace without which it would have no grounds upon which it could stand to begin with. In this light, the ultimate is nothing that lasts or is everlasting unless it is so contingent as to happen once and for all. Nor does it consist in opposing this life and the next, this world and the other world, the temporal and the eternal, much less in the classic opposition between the spiritual and the material, the good life and the goods of life.[9] It does not consist in changing worlds but in changing the world. It has a utopian rather than a sacral edge, as is actually illustrated by Paul's way of putting forward his Roman citizenship even though "here we have no lasting city" and even though "our commonwealth is in heaven."[10] Heaven: that which is no place but takes place when the religious is superseded by the secular and, conversely, when the secular is superseded by the religious. It even occurs on earth[11] whenever or wherever whatever you did you did not do in view of some "pie in the sky."[12]

As *eschatic* existence, faith is moreover to be lured neither by apocalypticism nor by historicism, neither by the catastrophism, millennial or otherwise, of the end of the world nor by the progressivism of salvation through some historical evolution from this world to the next. Insofar as faith lies at the juncture of commitment to God and involvement in the world, eschatic existence hangs on a worlding of the word. It hangs on a process whose threefold iteration is indicated by creation as the spacing of time, by incarnation as the timing of the eternal, and by the fullness of time as the overcoming of any gap between transcendence and immanence, between the holy and the secular. But then secular is only the name of that for which time, rather than becoming timeless, happens once and for all.

Eschatic existence, being then as autonomous as it is theonomous, is all the more vulnerable: it is alienated from itself as well as from God and driven into heteronomy by the joint antagonism of fundamentalism and secularism. If theonomy is the name for the religious method of putting the human into question, autonomy rightfully is its secular counterpart. Should we proceed further in this line of thought, I should gladly entertain the contention that, if theocracy is the religious name for anarchy, then anarchy is the secular name for theocracy—supposing that such vocables can still be trusted and then provided that, instead of some kind of arbitrary rule, human or divine, these vocables mean, each in its mode, that none of us is per se good enough to lord it over anyone else. No one. Not even God, so to speak.

God entrusts the creation to Adam—a move whose ultimate significance is woefully misconstrued if it is not viewed as entailing and combining both the desacralization of nature and the defatalization of history—in a word, the secularization of religion.

The human is no phenomenon exclusively emanating either from nature or from history. It makes sense only because it is at least as self-transcending as it is self-affirming. In the biblical tradition, it relates to God, to that which is emblematic of otherness in its radicality, yet without grinding that radicality into alienation whether from God or simply from other people, whatever their language. No God can be mine unless God can also be God for others. This explains why in the biblical tradition God is language rather than this or that. God need not be deified: the word becomes flesh.

Faith and the Adiaphoricity of the World

Neither polytheism nor atheism, much less secularism, has ever achieved such an iconoclastic conception of God. What language can attest, it can also test and contest. It deconstructs as well as it restructures and tempers physis with *nomos* as well as law with grace. Only language can spell the law, but then only so long as it does not fall short of grace. Giving to God what is God's and to Caesar what is Caesar's,[13] it surrenders neither to the supernatural nor to the natural.[14] All the more symbolic for being literal, it brings about the only world apt for being lived in by humans, amending and emending it, trimming and pruning it. Just as there would be no brain were it not for the mind, there would be no heart were it not for prayer, and no lips either were it not for language. But to the extent that language is what makes us human, we are its instrument. Being human consists in instrumenting language, under any of its guises.

Instrumenting language, the human is also an instrument of the divine, of the God that speaks, whereby the word is worlded: we speak to the extent that we are spoken for and are responsible for God as well as for the world. And speak we must: silence would tell either more than we would or less than we should. And just as an instrument needs to be kept clean, so lips and the heart need cleansing. To this end, the believer implores God, saying *munda cor meum ac labia mea* (purify my heart and my lips), as pointed out by Catherine Pickstock, who, commenting on this excerpt from the Roman liturgy of the Middle Ages, writes, "The heart and lips of the Deacon are worlded."[15] She even takes the trouble of reminding the reader that here "worlded" is to be heard in the sense of *munditia*, one of the noun forms of the verb *mundo* (to purify)! Astonishing the reader, she willfully neglects a gem—the fact that evidently from the same root are also derived the adjective *mundus* (pure, clean) and the noun *mundus* (world). In other words, no cleansing, no hallowing, and no worlding either except through that temporal synonym of "world," the *saeculum*.

Possibly, worldliness and otherworldliness, laden with negative connotations, still affect the religious imagination in general and piety in particular. One thing, however, rings loud and clear. They muted, perhaps, the biblical emphasis upon the covenant between God and all that is, upon a world so loved by God that he sends his only Son. But they never eclipsed either the covenant or God's love for the world. From Tertullian to Hegel and the death of God, "world" is a constant that furthermore invariably discriminates one theological discourse from another, provided that the cultural pregnancy of the Christian faith remains a sine qua non of its religious habilitation. In keeping with the biblical stress on the original goodness of creation, the otherworldly contempt for the world will in the course of history give way to the affirmation of the world. This paves the way for an ecological awareness of nature, not to mention the emergence of a world where everyone who comes or will come into the world has a right to a place in the sun, and where in other words radical innocence can be as fraudulent as the notion of original sin it has replaced.[16]

Yet even Tertullian, who died in 240, need not be decried more than he deserves. His way of equating *saeculum* and paganism or his contention that Athens and Jerusalem have nothing in common are certainly consonant with the rather arrogant otherworldliness abruptly displayed in his writings. Through his writings, however, and with equal composure, he further demonstrates his talent by goading the Christian faith into developing its own rhetoric and stocking it with its first conceptual tools. Nor does he, given the naturalism that pervades the paganism to which he reduces a bedeviled *saeculum*, shrink from contending that the soul is by nature Christian (*anima naturaliter christiana*). Bewildering! Yet coherent. He has sensed the religious dimension inherent in the secular.

If Athens and Jerusalem stand at opposite ends of the pole, this may mean only that what is at stake in their divergence actually deals but with the question on hand at that juncture—namely, what kind of religion will rightfully constitute the substance of culture? Even from the standpoint of the ultraconservative Tertullian, what is at stake deals with the cultural embodiment of the Christian faith, with its acculturation—and not its inculturation, a strategy developed of late by the Vatican and ascribing it to the role of a mole. What Tertullian is saying is not that culture is not a necessary form of religion, much less of true religion, but that no *given* culture is necessary per se and none exhausts religion. For example, when claiming that it did, Roman secularism leveled the charge of atheism at the Christians, or when realizing that it did not, Christianity was overtaken by the Greek legacy and somewhat hellenized throughout its love affair with metaphysics. Tertullian himself was pointing his finger at a soft spot: though suspicious of it, he nevertheless allows in turn for a suspicion to be levied on him. To wit: the *saeculum* is precisely what paganism and Christianity have in common.

Muted by Tertullian, this is an insight whose credibility becomes more and more persuasive even before Augustine. In *The City of God*, the latter's other magnum opus, it would even seem that not only was Tertullian being understood better than he understood himself, but that Augustine's vision of the relation between Athens and Jerusalem amounts to a deconstruction of their alleged opposition. For the epistemological bent of Tertullian's ill-secured fideism Augustine substitutes a phenomenologically oriented dialectic of the word become flesh,[17] of that which, for being eternal, is no less standing in the now, in that which has no past.[18] For Tertullian's provocative notion of the absurd, he substitutes the no-less-challenging if equally paradoxical notion of grace, which, as Thomas Aquinas will later assert, does not abrogate nature but perfects it.

Paganism, Augustine contends, may well have been shot through with vices, but they were "splendid." In this way "natural man" is both asserted and challenged: no human being is natural except through grace. In contrast to the prevailing assumption of natural being as sinful being, there is emerging with Augustine more than a hint to the effect that to sin is to go against nature.[19] Should he, on the contrary, appear at times to identify paganism with secularism, this only goes to show that secularism is merely the effect of an otherworldly puritanism, of which, generally, Augustine steers clear. "It is," he writes, "the peculiarity of secularism that it worships a god or gods, by whose aid it may reign victorious in temporal peace, animated not with the love of wise counsel but with the lust for possession. For the good use this world in order that they may enjoy God; but the evil use God in order that they may enjoy this world."[20]

Clearly, whatever the merits of Augustine's case, the point he wants to make is not that for the good, God comes first, and for the evil, only secondarily if at all. The point is not that God comes first, as the evil think who therefore use God in order to enjoy the world, but that God comes *down* all the while the world is being and must be used in order for God to be enjoyed. The world is what the city of God and the city of "man" have in common, even to the extent, Augustine keeps saying, that they are "interwoven as it were in this present transitory world, and mingle with one another."[21] Between them what will make the difference is the church, not as principle of segregation but of hallowing God throughout the world. If with Tertullian Christians tend to form a society within society, this is no longer the case with Augustine. The church must instead mesh with society.

From the standpoint of Jesus, the secular is what Israel has in common with the nations. It is also what implicitly the early Christians thought they might have in common with the other religions of the empire. Though persecuted, they had no problem with the pluralism officially endorsed by the Roman authorities. They had a problem only with the cost of it.[22] They neither could nor would worship the emperor along with God and were outlawed: to say the least, pluralism had its limits from the imperial standpoint and possibly from their own standpoint, too. But then it seems safe to assume that pluralism as such is not what the early Christians rejected. It is the religion of it. Their case is clear. Not only does it call for dedivinizing the emperor; it also aims at secularizing the uppermost beacon of civil authority.

In keeping with the biblical formula "from faith to faith," faith extends into faith, but no instance of it has primacy over another. Every instance lies equally close to and is equally distant from its core. Because what faith requires has no *archē* of its own, it is as "an-archic" as God's demand is holy. The same applies to the secular in relation to which faith is but the far side. The secular is ultimately at stake in the worlding of the word, and in turn this very worlding itself calls for a secularizing process whose affirmation it carries but only as one—hallowing being the other—prong of the eschatological dialectic so typical of the biblical tradition. Holiness and the secular, hallowing and secularization, go hand in hand. So do anarchy and theocracy, bizarre though this may sound. But more than a hint of this basic compatibility of the holy and the secular lurks behind various facets of the biblical tradition, ranging from the very idea of a chosen—though fundamentally undeserving—people to Paul's at once anarchic and theocratic contention that in Christ there is neither Greek nor Jew, male nor female, master nor slave.[23]

This eschatic dimension of faith, considerably dimmed later on or diverted time and again, nevertheless has since Augustine and his reinterpretation of the legacies of Athens and Jerusalem probed the Christian tradition and marked it indelibly. Even if only with hindsight, *sub specie aeternitatis*, the eschatic dimension accounts for an enduring conception of the church that, despite shortcomings, keeps displaying an ethic that ultimately hangs on an affirmation no less gratuitous for affirming that all is grace.

This is not to say, once again, that "amazing grace" never gave way to cheaper versions serving only to camouflage structural arrogance, whether institutional or conceptual, as evinced by such notions of the church as sole means of salvation or as window dressing of holier-than-thou congregations. When the truth that makes us free[24] becomes the monopoly of a language, then that language does not tell the truth. No truth is the monopoly of a language. Rather than being unveiled by language, it unveils language. No sooner is it spoken than it disowns any language and yet comes into its own through language. How it is said is more important than what is said about it.²⁵ Otherwise, we are the elect and others are damned, just as, in the "natural" order, what sets us free often is what others are oppressed by.

We are not cast all in the same mold, to be sure. Nor do we need to be so cast for all of us to be at an equal distance from one another. That is what, here, is called anarchy: it is consonant with theocracy, when God is at an equal distance from all.²⁶ What anarchy and theocracy have in common is no doubt some kind of utopianism rooted in human nature, if not in nature *tout court*. More precisely, this is a utopianism that is rooted in language rather than in nature, in the nostalgic idea of some natural harmony. Utopia is neither the good old days nor a pipe dream. It points to just what is at stake in the transformation of ice into an igloo, of the environment (*Umwelt*) into a world (*Welt*). In order to be made hospitable, the environment need not be inhospitable. It need only be indifferent. So also can we be indifferent to one another instead of being one another's keeper. Cain knew what he was talking about: the natural bond was not enough to make him his brother's keeper.²⁷ From opposite directions, this is a point that both anarchy and theocracy stress, though perhaps each with a different kind of vengeance. Just as today, in the so-called war against terrorism, we are caught between some kind of theocracy, on the one hand, and anarchy, on the other, so far as, while the rhetoric for waging this war is internationally couched, the strategy for implementing it is not.

Saying that no one, though possibly good enough to govern oneself, is good enough to govern another could, putting it another way, say what anarchy and theocracy have in common and point at the same time to what distinguishes them. The democratic pattern of social policy to which they each lay claim is also what—through their respective implementation—places them at opposite ends of the spectrum. But there, what it brings to light is that the anarchic pattern of social convention rests in its appeal not so much to absolute freedom (neither God nor master) as to an a-theocracy of sorts or, in a more positive mood, a democracy without confession of sins. By contrast, so long as sin is not only an individual but also a social category, any pretense of a theocratic straitjacket put on society is bound to be subverted and stranded by the principle that no one is good enough to govern another. So far as they shed light on democracy, theocracy differs from anarchy, at least, to the extent that—paraphrasing W. H. Auden's poetic interpretation of Reinhold Niebuhr's definition—true democracy begins with a free confession of sins.

There is no need here to delve into the roots of democracy. For our purposes, let us observe that, in contrast to American democracy, European democracies make no such claim as "In God we trust," or "One nation under God." Yet in a drastic, sudden reversal of political theory, Germany and France, not to mention the Vatican, have recently admitted to collective guilt and made a public confession of it. Acknowledging guilt and confessing sins need not be confused, of course. And that is precisely the point. When, in the middle of the last century, Picasso wants to paint *Guernica*, he first goes and studies Grünewald's *Crucifixion* in Colmar. He already knew: we live in a world in which God can no longer be taken for granted. It is of no matter whether this world is construed in theistic or in atheistic terms. Whether democracy invokes God or no God, the heart of the matter is that the world in which we live affords no meaning unless this meaning displays a concern that is secular enough to be common to all of us. Call this world pluralistic or by any other name, above all it cannot spell God except on secular terms: neither in the rigid and bellicose sense of the secular into which these terms were twisted by modernity, nor according to the self-flagellating or exorcist's use of it in today's postmodern climate. Spelling God is indeed foreclosed, except in the light of the least erring approach to a world without other moorings than are afforded from words, a fiction, a mere language. Accordingly, more important than any notion of cultural pluralism or religious diversity is what I would call—with Winquist and still in the wake of Saint Paul—the adiaphoricity of the world.[28] It is but another way of designating the secular as arena of faith, however this faith is understood and construed.

In view of an ethic for *this* world, at one time or another the average version of the Christian faith has been assessed by subordinating its kernel to either a notion of natural law or a story of salvation, or both. In fact, it was thwarted. Christian faith was bent into an ethic for the other world, a world beyond this world. It subdued the eschatological dimension of the incarnation. But it continued throbbing with the expectation of a new heaven and a new earth. It somehow refrained from muffling the groaning of the creation or from dousing the world yearning for its worldhood, for its hallowing. In time, eroding its supernatural aspect, even this traditional ethic of faith overcomes otherworldliness and is focused on the world as theater of the glory of God. As Calvin puts it in keeping with an unrelenting biblical injunction, the earth is the Lord's, and therefore belonging to no one but the Lord, it can belong to anyone and not just to a happy few.

Biblical religion is not a territorial (henotheistic) religion. In contrast to religions that sacralize the land, biblical religion desacralizes it and, hallowing the name of God, spreads this name over the face of the whole earth. Not always convincingly, to be sure. The story of the church is an endless concatenated confession of sins. It includes institutional pride and megalomania as well as contemptible devotion to a no-less-devotional contempt for the world and for the body. Not to mention racism and sexism, it includes a deceptive promotion of otherworldliness. Under the guise of life after death, it even covers up a lucrative materialism and its attending, procedural system of salvation (prepaid or postpaid, depending on the indulgence purchased). Still, even as André Malraux would say, cathedrals were built and tombs erected. Heavenly destiny began here and now. The church praises God, and, however timidly, it affirms and settles in the world. The day comes when nothing is more receptive to the praise of God than the secular.

Only through the secular can God be praised and God's name hallowed. Conversely, an ethic of hallowing is an ethic that, restoring the world to its worldhood, honors the secular.[29] Just as the eternal is not what comes before or after time, so also the church comes neither before nor after the world. Again, only through the secular alone can God be ascribed the kingdom and the power and the glory—*in saecula saeculorum,* forever and ever, so long as the secular does not last but happens *once and for all.* The secular calls not for heroes but for saints.

Saints are not heroes faced with inexorable fate, much less are they fetish-like figureheads conjuring an indefectible social order. They are ordinary characters, but their characteristic lies not in any display of power but in their powerlessness, in the fiction of power, in turning power into a fiction of the real, with no more power than the power of words. No world is for them more ideal than the real world so far as it is a world contained and ordained by language rather than by power and the silence it imposes all around. Just as at the mouth of the body, lips turn into words—words that may upset the applecart of social, moral, spiritual conventions and the like.

Attention to this character of the saint is drawn, among others, by Michel Walzer's now-classic *Revolution of the Saints* and by Edith Wyschogrod's perceptive and groundbreaking study *Saints and Postmodernism*. What they bring to light is an image of the saint more consonant with the secular than with the religious dimension of life. Popular adulation or supernatural devotion notwithstanding, a saint's life is geared less to heaven than to this world. It is geared to heaven insofar as it measures up to the world. It brings heaven down to earth.

Saints are "ordinary" people: they are ordained to reconfigure the order of things, though by no power of their own. Power is not shared. It is personified and ranks people into masters and slaves. Sharing is not a matter of us and them but of I and Thou, brought together through nothing but the aura of words—unlike power—so precarious as to be shared by all in whose respect saints personify nothing. They really are not even persons. They are personages (such as are characteristic of a drama). Appearing on time as others appear on stage, they are so contemporaneous with the world at a given time of its history that they bear witness to the fact that the basic experience of life, historically outdated as soon as it is dated, lies no more in being dated than in being outdated. With inimitable style, Malraux had, half a century ago, seeded this notion in preparing the ground for his studies of "Great Historical Figures." He called them "historical," but, take note, he was all the more conscious of the fact that they stood out of history. They stood up to it. They withstood all unfurling of self-fulfilling history, Hegelian or otherwise. Instead of a world judged by its history, instead of a world weaned on history, theirs is a world no longer told by the sound and fury of history but reconfigured in view of a still-untold future and staged and enacted through fictions of a language all the more efficient for being powerless. Great and so-called historical figures judge, not the world, social or otherwise, but the ideological fiction on which it is weaned.

If, likewise, a saint's life is a judgment, it is a judgment on the church, not on the world. Regardless of how the church defines itself theologically, it is itself a fiction of its own language. More precisely, it is a fiction of its own liturgical structure, a structure through which church and world are the two sides of one and the same coin. They are brought and liturgically belong together just as, through the Christ, the divine and the human are brought together. But the communion of saints, by which the church identifies itself, in spite of its liturgical interface with the world, gradually prompts the church to turn its back on the world. By thus relegating the secular to a subordinate position, the church surrenders, in fact, to the religious. By standing for so religious a communion, it dissolves into an otherworldly mystical entity. Thinking it is in this way ahead of the world, it in fact lags behind it. It drives a wedge between the old and the new, tradition and innovation, the religious and the secular, or, symbolically speaking, between Greek and Jew.

Again this last point takes us back to Paul and his contention that in Christ there is neither Jew nor Greek. It also reminds us of James Joyce and his equally pregnant amalgamation of Jew and Greek. Reupholstering an obsolescent Christian tradition, he berates it for being tossed to and fro between the Hebraic spirituality of its religious dimension and the Greek mentality of its cultural dimension. These dimensions the Christian tradition so parsimoniously commingles with one another that, hampered by rather than freed from the classic opposition of body and soul, it oscillates between the two prongs of its understanding of the dynamics of faith. Religion is either Jewish or Greek. And so, because the Christian tradition fails to overcome this dichotomy, some still go on adhering to it. They are sundered and pitted against themselves. Instead of pulverizing the opposition of Jew and Greek, they interiorize it. In a superfluous quest for identity, they go on wondering whether they are Greek somatically and Jewish psychologically, or the other way around. They do not realize that, in Christ, the roots of identity are not to be sought in nature or in history but in that grace of God through which being human becomes natural to the human being.

Greek or Jewish, we are heroes of sorts. Saints are not. They are not what they are by mere comparison with others. Heroes, in fact, go by the rules; unlike most of us, they look exceptional and, eventually, exemplary enough to be imitated. Heroes put up with this world: it is all that is the case, and so does it remain at least for the rest of us. But heroes only change worlds. By contrast, saints do not. But they radically alter our perception of the world: the world itself can be changed. But then this calls for another kind of ethic than ultimately one of resignation to some immutable order of things.

In order to catch a glimpse of such an ethic, we must, writes Wyschogrod, "look not to some opposite of ethics but elsewhere, to life narratives, especially those of saints." Smile not. Whether these saints have actually lived or not makes no difference for her. What she is concerned with is not the object of a saint's devotion or commitment but the narrative of a life that, even fanned into surreal hagiographies, fodders a fiction. Similarly, the important thing is not whether, as per rules and regulations, they were canonized or not. What matters is that, whether religious or secular, they were *dissenters,* and that while subverting their own tradition, they recovered its intention by charting a new challenge to the normative structures of its moral theory.[30]

Saints do not seek merely to change worlds, they change the world. For that there is no recipe—and no rules, either—but faith alone. Though spent throughout a lifetime seeking for a rule by which to live and die,[31] faith creates no precedent, even with the life of a saint; it harks back to no antecedent, either. It will even show that as soon as a rule is formulated, this rule, so long as it is meant to be enforced, can at best only be considered legal and, as such, is hence tolerated.[32] And tolerance makes no sense unless it calls for a review of the object initially intended by a rule.

Rules are symbolic. They cease to be applicable unless they keep showing how the respective demands of the universal and the singular—not unlike those of the religious and the secular—can coincide with one another. When they fail to achieve this end (because symbol cannot be enforced), they can only expect to be observed—religiously. Rules compensate for the failure of religion, just as, according to Nietzsche, clinging to Christian morality attempts to make up for the demise of God. Whether this attempt is in vain or not, it is not so much the religious dimension of morality that is lost as its secular dimension. Appearances to the contrary notwithstanding, what is lost is the secular—the worldhood of the world. What is lost is that paramount notion of the worldhood of a world created and brought to light through the worlding of the word. What is lost is that passion for a world without which God is not God—because God is a God that makes room for the world, as the religious makes room for the secular. Incarnation is in this respect but a repetition (in Kierkegaard's sense) of creation. God is not God without the world, but the world is not God: it does not mistake its worldhood for the kingdom of God. Nor does it, in the name of a pretended radical immanentism, relegate transcendence to a realm above and beyond this world.

In the biblical tradition, it is not religion that binds us to one another. Nor is it religion that "contains" the world. It is God. The world, either in its religious or in its secular dimension, is but the empty tomb of a language of which religion, disestablished and secularized, is the ultimate fiction, or the parable. But the parable of what? Of nothing but a world falling into place out of nothing. Of a world for which God is no stopgap.

The death of God is the secret of religion. It is also the secret of biblical religion, except that this religion is not focused on a God that dies in order to be born again. It is focused on a God that speaks—no sooner worshipped than turned into an idol: no God is God, let alone the world. The world is what it is—an effect of language—and to this basic adiaphoricity of the world corresponds the gratuitousness of God. Or else the world would be God, and the real would cease to be symbolic. The merit of biblical religion is, in this respect, that it is endowed with an imaginary that is not at odds with the symbols of its rhetoric much less with its real world. Brute facts do not think. They are neutral and, though their effect can be positive or negative, they make up that sphere of technicalities (strawberries do not grow on ice) on which is predicated the adiaphoricity of the world.

The world does not point to God, though it should. It should point to God, but it does not. The reality of God is granted with the reality of the world, and yet it cannot be taken for granted, much less by those chosen to trust in it. And even so ambiguous an expression is not fortuitous. It depicts our *post mortem dei*, postmodern, situation, not the least paradox of which is that, even in its triumphalist wing of deconstruction theory, it is all the more culturally biblical if not Christian for being post-Christian. Clearly, postmodern thinking exhibits affinities with the iconoclasm of biblical discourse and, somehow, even depends on it.

The question facing postmodern thinking is whether it is as committed to the secular as is claimed. Any affirmative answer is vexed by still another question. Jaspers tackled it by suggesting his notion of a philosophical faith. Considering faith a mode of being, he disestablished religion—short of secularizing it. Postmodern thinkers would, in contrast, rather more readily evoke the sacred, as though that were all that was left of faith after the death of God. There is no compensation for it. To fall back on the sacred is to fall back on a revved-up version of some denominator supposedly held in common by all religions, regardless of their particular territorial manifestations. Possibly the sacred makes up for the repudiation of a supernatural conception of transcendence. But is compensation all that our world needs? Does it not, rather, need a new language? In a deregulated world such as ours, though virtually desacralized by its technology yet haunted still by the imperialism of religion, and all the more crying for tolerance, what we all have in common is the secular.

Inklings of the Secular

Meshing with society, the church cannot fulfill its obligation without being imperiled at the same time by allowing for the political reality of faith to be superseded by some worldly *Realpolitik*. For instance, under Charlemagne the church becomes so identified with his *imperium* that *ecclesia* in fact designates not the church but the empire itself. A questionable solution, whether rejected or not, its only merit probably lies in the sole fact that it never presumed to be the "final solution," whether under the aegis of a would-be theocratic fundamentalism or of a forerunner of some secularist ideology. History shows that, at home with neither, the church itself subsequently manages on the whole to withstand both temptations. Besides, its understanding of the relation between religion and culture develops not in terms of an opposition between church and world but in terms of a dialectic, religiously as well as culturally more intimate to the real core of the problem, the relation between *Corpus Christi* and *corpus christianum*. That is, a dialectic between the worlding of the word and the worldhood of the world, between the religious and the secular.

At the apex of the Middle Ages, pope and emperor, challenging one another, compete for supremacy. The church manifests its supremacy by defining itself as the body of Christ and thus the better subordinating the world to its rule, yet without going so far as to absorb it. On the contrary, drawing a line between reason and revelation, between philosophical and theological truth, Thomas Aquinas will draw a line between the religious and the secular. Not a Berlin wall, to be sure. But it is a division rigid enough in its consequences for dissenting voices to sound forth and be raised, especially—and no less ironically—from among the more "religious" pool of the church and, strangely enough, within the spiritual wing of the ecclesial structure. This, in an age when "nothing would seem to be more otherworldly and apolitical—indeed, downright idealistic—than the doctrine that because Christ, Mary, and the apostles had practiced total poverty," one would expect that "it was incumbent on the church to obey their example and to abstain from owning anything." No one expected less than that. But "by one of those curious ironies with which history and perhaps especially the history of the church is fraught, this otherworldly position formed an alliance with various secularists of the fourteenth century, who were asserting the authority of the state over against that of the church."[33] With arguments culled from as devoted a churchman as William of Ockham, "the emperor and his supporters cast themselves in the role of liberators of the true church from the burdens of property and power." Doubtless, the emperor was stretching Ockham's views.

Two things, however, must be noted. One is that these are views that reverberate an image of Jesus that Ockham shares with his fellow

Franciscans. The other is that, already with Ockham himself, civil power emanates neither from God nor from nature but from the people. The upshot of this leaps to the eye: with this image of Jesus, what is achieved is "a contribution to the formulation of the founding principles and 'secular values' of modern political philosophy."[34]

But the ideology of salvation and its changing-worlds motif still holds, though not perhaps in as dualistic a mood as with Tertullian. It continues to control the texture of the good life and its ramifications into the various goals of human existence, whether ultimate or penultimate, individual or social, spiritual or temporal. But it has not, if only because of its roots, abated the biblical concern for the worldhood of the world, though this concern was now being held in ontological abeyance by the metaphysical turn of Christian thought. This is a concern that evinces two aspects, both of which stem from Augustine's dialectic of the two cities and, by way of Saint Thomas on the one hand and of William of Ockham on the other, are woven, though perhaps unequally, into the fabric of the Reformation or at least some segments of it. Indeed, one of these aspects bears the stamp of the sacramentarian, while the other stands for the charismatic approach to the secular or worldhood of the world. The former subordinates the world to the church. The latter, considering this world as the sole arena of faith, accordingly views the church as a principle of social novation.

Most instrumental in this respect is the concept of vocation, whether in its medieval version as a calling to the priesthood or in its enlargement through the reformers' doctrine of the priesthood of all believers. At first a marker of spiritual mobility (by way of the church), vocation anticipates and will soon show the way to the modern principle of social mobility. Spilling over the spiritual sphere, it will affect every walk of life, regardless of one's position or profession. Entailing a subtle critique of the established church socially as well as spiritually, this move was doubtless facilitated by the mystical wing of Christianity; unquestionably, it is also boosted by the emerging monastic orders, each of them emblematic of a small-scale utopia, bent on changing the world by first changing the church. This is precisely what the reformers will seek to do. And they know how they benefit from the fact that, in sundry walks of life, forerunners had not been missing. For example, until the fourteenth century, Saint James the Less is represented with the fuller's tool with which he was tortured. By the end of the Middle Ages, however, crafts and trades had all so evolved that society had to reflect their effects. The fuller's tool of Saint James's martyrdom was now antiquated. It is replaced by the most recent carder's instrument.[35] In similar fashion, we move from the church as mystical body to the church as principle of social novation when the Last Judgment scene of a cathedral's classical tympanum is replaced on a tympanum like that of the basilica of Avioth by the figures and emblems representing the various crafts and trades making up society.

Luther and especially Calvin will rely and bet on this charismatic approach to the secular. Luther, however, continues to adhere to the dichotomous theory of two realms (religious and secular, private and public). He also holds the view that one can and need only serve God *in* whatever calling or function one happens to fill. A prince must accordingly govern as should a prince rather than a Christian. In 1520, barely two or three years after posting his ninety-five theses, Luther still is of the opinion that the civil authorities should—and therefore could—summon a church council.

It is Calvin who will explore in a more dynamic fashion this overlapping of religious community and civil society. Rather than *in vocatione* (in keeping with one's calling), it is regardless of—yet through—one's vocation (*per vocationem*) that one is to serve God, should it for that purpose have to be changed. Meanwhile, mayor and minister, so to speak, are equally vicars of Christ and according to their own respective functions. As Karl Holl stated it in his famous dictum, the Reformation consists in secularizing religion and in spiritualizing culture. More specifically, as Ernst Cassirer will assess it, "The Reformation seems to agree with the Renaissance in giving new value and new sanction to life on earth. It, too, calls for a spiritualization of the content of faith; and this spiritualization is not confined to the ego, the religious subject, but encompasses also the being of the world, placing a new relation to the basis of religious certainty. The world is now to be justified on grounds of the certainty of faith. Thus again the ascetic demand for negation of this world is met by a demand for world affirmation, that is, in certainty within the secular order."[36] Cassirer's emphasis on certainty entails an ethic for the secular that goes beyond Max Weber's identification of this ethic as innerworldly asceticism in contrast to the otherworldly asceticism of the Middle Ages—though the intention is well taken.

But if medieval otherworldly asceticism had to cope with a world marred by scarcity, it must be noted that, in the aftermath of the Reformation and the Renaissance and in view of the industrial and scientific revolutions that will ensue, abundance rather than scarcity is what looms on the horizon as being in need of stewardship. Not to mention the fact that, somehow, asceticism sounds more religious than secular, self-limiting frugality would better describe the fundamental principle of the Protestant ethic, should for that purpose a label be needed at all. Asceticism remains the hallmark of a life hemmed in by scarcity; frugality harks back to the biblical injunction according to which social justice and solidarity cannot be achieved unless the rich "have nothing over" and the poor have "no lack,"[37] unless life abundant is available to all who, regardless of where they come from, should be reduced to "hoping against hope."[38]

Even the notion of salvation cannot quite survive the impact of the Reformation on the secularization of religion. Although no ablation of it is advocated frontally, it will, at least substantially, recover its biblical orientation. Already with Luther's faith and its thoroughgoing self-examination, the heretofore basic question "What must I do in order to be saved" gives way to "Who or what kind of God is this God who saves me?" Luther's insight amounts to a virtual shaking of the foundations of traditional religion. In his treatise on Christian liberty, he writes, "Quite voluntarily and without recompense the Christian does all that he does without thereby seeking his own advantage or salvation. What is done is done just to please God thereby."[39] Faith lies in being released from the very obsession of salvation—an idea that, strange as it may sound, is embedded in Calvin's doctrine of predestination. Losing at all events its ontological moorings, salvation is recast in relational terms, and faith turns into a mode of being: the believer himself or herself is, according to Luther, a Christ unto his or her neighbor. Using an image from Tillich, one is compelled to observe that the vertical already lies in the horizontal. Or that transcendence consists in making room for that which is immanent.

As grandiose an idea as this may have been in its conception, it will however give way or subsequently fall prey to a drive toward a would-be radical immanentism more aptly described as an immanentism with a vengeance. Always lurking on the horizon of Western culture, it never was as ominous as it will henceforth be, when theology itself is in fact either driven out of the church or so domesticated by the church that Schleiermacher himself will barely succeed in reanimating it in his attempt to disarm the cultural despisers of religion. But by then theology has for all practical purposes already bifurcated into law and civil polity on the one hand, and into law and political philosophy on the other. The gap that had for long been yawning between the church and the world, between faith and culture, will not only widen, it will result in artificially pitting the religious and the secular one against the other and meretriciously plaguing them both accordingly.

Consider, in this respect, the "idealism" of Hegel. Not to mention Kant on one side and Heidegger on the other, with roots going back to Luther, what is this idealism actually concerned with if not the worldhood of the world—its secularity? Denouncing the otherworldliness of the established church and what he calls its "sacramental materialism," Hegel displays nonetheless an amazing fondness for such classical, if not worn out, expressions as the invisible church or, for that matter, the kingdom of God. And what do they mean? They simply mean that the reality of God is at stake in the reality of the world: if no God is God, no world is without God. The world is like a manger, in which lies but one for whom there is no room in the inn, in the church. Coping with the world, as though it were its trust, the invisible church has indeed little to do with the visible church. But here we must go back to Calvin.

Calvin similarly castigates all those for whom the kingdom of God lies tucked away in some heavenly realm instead of paving the way toward the "true country." Retrieved from the substantialized metaphysical order of an otherworldly salvation, the church is now geared to the task of changing the world, to the extent that Calvin's ecclesiology reads more like a declaration of political theology than like a mystical treatise about a community sheltered and segregated from the world. At the risk of an oversimplification, we move from the *imperium* as essence of the church to the church as a matter of civil government. It is not that the religious and the secular are confused with one another. Rather, they will court such a confusion if, left to their own devices, they drift into either fundamentalism or secularism as the case may be. The separation of church and state is a matter of pragmatic reflective equilibrium, traumatically lost sight of as soon as one ideology is pitted against the other in battles so dubious as to vouch for nothing short of mutual extermination. Power, whether religious or secular, becomes tyrannical and arbitrary unless it limits itself.

Calvin was a lawyer. Taking the measure of the new situation to whose insemination Calvin contributed, Michael Walzer writes most judiciously:

"Religion produced a counterpolity to the state; as a prelude to admitting the state to the world of religion, Calvin admitted politics to religion. He often described the church as a commonwealth and the metaphor is a significant key to his thought."[40] Certainly, the metaphor was not missed by John Cotton, the Puritan divine, who writes, "It is necessary that all power on earth be limited, church power or other. . . . It is counted [by some] a matter of danger to the state to limit prerogatives; but it is a further danger not to have them limited. . . . And it is meet that magistrates in the Commonwealth and officers in the church should [each] desire to know the utmost bounds of their own [respective spheres of] power."[41] What follows from a view like this is no less significant.

Having to cope with a commonwealth, no particular church is the church. Denominations do not exhaust the reality of the church, and no less significant is the fact that, on the American scene, the notion of a holy commonwealth upstages that of a holy church. Nor do, for that matter, denominations altogether exhaust the scope of religion, much less that of faith, especially since denominations are but debris of a church held on a leash by some territory, of territorial churches now still confined within an area but stretching, archipelago fashion, across an ocean swept by tradewinds of diverse persuasions. What denominations have in common is nothing but the secular, which explains why they can merge when the configurations of the secular undergo a drastic change and theological differences lose their ground. This also explains why new religions today can blossom and thrive on the religious veneer *already* spread on the secularized mind-set to which they appeal.

Nearly half a century ago, while President Eisenhower, expressing his confidence in whatever future, was declaring that "our Government is based on a deeply felt religious faith," Will Herberg was describing the American people as being at once the most religious and the most secular. Nearly two millennia earlier, the apostle Paul described a similar situation by saying that the world is full of gods.[42] Unlike Paul, who—I tend to think—cared what kind of gods these were, Eisenhower, in a mood no doubt less apostolic than political, proudly went overboard and, enthusiastically brimming over with this deeply felt religious faith, scuttled it by then saying "I don't care what it is." Brutal, surely. Sobering, too. Like life, the secular can be brutal. And, one would surmise, it is brutal only because or to the extent that, correspondingly, religion has become vulgar—as Nietzsche would say.

It is Nietzsche who points out that, after the collapse of Christian culture, what remains is the Bible. By this he means not a book but a trace—the emblematic trace of a language, if not of language *tout court*. What remains is a theology of language, the cutting edge of discourse reduced neither to the religious nor to the secular. Indeed, faith is what religion and the secular have in common, regardless of the respective metamorphoses they undergo even while, through a series or process of renewed mutual articulations, they come to terms with one another and hinge one upon the other—world without end, throughout the ages, *in saecula saeculorum*.

Christianity never really lost sight of the secular but was blinded by it. The biblical process of secularization reasserted by the Christian tradition bifurcated. Secularism outwits secularity, and the drive toward the secular is overshadowed by the mystical interpretation of the incarnation.

No God Is God

Incarnation and the Secular

O inexpressible mystery
and unheard of paradox:
the Intangible is touched;
the Eternal Word becomes
accessible to our speech.
The Timeless steps into time;
the Son of God becomes
the Son of Man.

—Gregory of Nyssa, fourth century

Only a god could make us believe in God did this god
not lie in our own flesh.

—Michel Henry, *C'est moi la vérité: Pour une
philosophie du christianisme*

Not God but the word becomes flesh and is worlded. It lies in the secular. Radicalizing the immanence of the world and the transcendence of God, secularization is and has always been the necessary yet seldom acknowledged alternative to the mystical interpretation of the body of Christ.

Basically if crudely put, two general patterns would seem to account for the classic approaches to the incarnation. As described by Marco Maria Olivetti, the incarnation is either construed in terms of a "body" "animated" by a "spiritual principle" or it is focalized on the notion of a "God who becomes man."[1] Each approach has two components, which are so related to one another that this relation is articulated, in one case, from within and, in the other, from without. Though cast in more or less mystical terms, one approach sparks off ethical concerns, while the other is finally swayed by the latent proclivity of its premises toward an ontological elaboration. In short, the incarnation is viewed from below in one instance and, in the other, from above. Outwardly, if at all, these two patterns do seem to differ from one another. Still, it is a moot question whether there is so fundamental a difference between them.

Worlding the Word: Incarnation and the Christ

After all, the presuppositions to which either approach harks back are of a similar nature. Whether the incarnation is construed from above or from below, it presumes some degree of necessary complementarity between the two components of each set, that is, between body and spirit on the one hand and between God and "man" on the other. But then, what both patterns overlook is that, fastened on such an assumption of complementarity, they tone down and even imperil or shake off the very notion of God's radical otherness. Neither pattern is susceptible any longer to this otherness, which is radical only because it rests on, and demands, not complementarity but compatibility—the mutual enfranchisement of the components paired in their respective sets, and not their annexation or the alienation of one component by the other. Alien is indeed that person who is denied rights and privileges enjoyed by others, often exempted of duties and obligations that stem from such privileges. To be alienated is to be deprived of one's otherness. Defied is all respect for mutual otherness, for what—not to speak of social justice—even love calls for. Even God can love only that which is not God. Self-love is not love. Nor is even love merely a matter of sex. Ultimately it is a matter of words and involves not mere complementarity but compatibility—as in fact is the case with a poem made up with words, or again as is the case with two human beings concerned with being human through love.

Complementarity implies that two elements can relate to one another because they are, say physiologically, meant for one another. Compatibility implies that they can, though they are not meant to. Between them, even as for Kierkegaard between the divine and the human, there is an infinite qualitative difference, which can never be reduced to a matter of quantity: God, as the saying used to go, is not "man" written in capital letters. No sooner is this warning forgotten than the incarnation ceases to be the deterrent it is supposed to be, whether against dualism on the one hand or against monism on the other. Both dualism and monism rest on a complementary understanding of the relation between the divine and the human as well as between man and woman. They appeal to the notion of a difference. But whether this difference is upheld and asserted or toned down, it is merely quantitative, framed according to a plus-and-minus scale, as implied even by Kierkegaard's a contrario insistence on the infinite qualitative dimension of this difference. Whatever difference is alleged between the two classical approaches to the incarnation, the point is that, like creation, incarnation is a matter of language—a fact that both these approaches tend to forget.

Olivetti himself is doubtless quite aware of this. When he points out that it is not the body per se that is "animated" by a spiritual principle, he means that it is only what lies, as it were, between body and spirit that makes a difference, and that this difference is to be appraised in terms not of complementarity but of compatibility. This point becomes even more clear when we recall the way in which Barth himself, among others, contends that, precisely when the word becomes flesh, it is not Jesus's human reality as such that is the object of revelation. For Barth, as already noted by Henri Bouillard, "The incarnation of the Word is not a state but a divine act."[2] It takes place—though no place is specific to it—and is less a location than a site, a centrifugal communications turntable that, as on the Web, bonds us with one another yet without tying us up. The word becomes flesh. The word bodies forth, and God "becomes man."

God is not God without us. Therefore, no God is God and no flesh in and of itself is life itself. All flesh is but only the necessary if ephemeral condition of life—the ultimate as well as unique occasion of the contingency and hence of the fullness of life. Life is what happens through the flesh; but although without the flesh life would not take place, flesh is per se not life. Nor can the flesh stand in lieu of life. It "places" but, of itself, can never replace life. It can only invest itself in that which it is not—in life. Otherwise, life would be a makeshift of the flesh. Or it would be reduced to the flesh, reduced to biology, reduced to that which, being only its recipients, we could not receive unless and until we have acknowledged it as a gift. Because this gift is one that we neither do nor have to deserve, it is all the more demanding—like language, through which we are spoken for.

To such a demand we must respond, and we can do so only if we respond to it with our whole being. Lips are turned into words that give mouth to the body[3] and flesh it out through that which it is not—the spirit without which the flesh would never "become" the word. Being embodied is no imposition but a disposition. It is not a possession. One comes into one's own through that which one does not own. No body is mine if only because nobody can or is ever meant to be owned by anyone. No poet owns the language that inhabits her or him. Nor do I own that through which, flesh or spirit, I come into my own, regardless of my skin, my race and color, or my religion—and God knows that my innermost self runs no deeper than my skin. I have no body other than that through which the word inhabits me or, again, that through which I am claimed by the spirit who, in Paul's view of the body, makes it a temple of God.[4] And then I am housed. But I am housed in language—not shelled in, as a snail would be; that is, I am exposed to that which I am not, whether other people or the world, or God.

In other words, caught between flesh and spirit, we are, even through our body, in the hands of language. Being spoken for, we can neither posit no God as God nor deny that no God is God. Even God is in the hands of language, and the relationship between God and the human is therefore predicated on their mutual otherness rather than on some dialectic of identity and difference. This relationship is funded by one and the same language, which they have in common, and yet they are distinguished by it, even brought into question by it.

With respect to the human side, one must bear in mind that the term "flesh" designates "religious and moral man insofar as he undertakes to accomplish or to secure his salvation [and that, accordingly,] the 'flesh' is not opposed to the spirit of man, but to the work of God in Jesus Christ for the salvation of men,"[5] as the tradition was wont to say. To the extent, however, that God is language and this work of God is carried through the word become flesh (and God as well as the human are accordingly in the hands of language), what the flesh is opposed to, or seeks to escape from, whether through the ministrations of nature or those of history, is the verbal character of the divine as well as the human condition. Being human is no datum either of flesh or of spirit but is their mutual embodiment, that is, an extension if not an intensification of the self as that which happens and, being present once and for all, occupies no space, sacred or otherwise. Embodiment is not a sacralizing of this or that but a timing of the self.[6]

This timing is what we call a body, and much like a clock this body is nevertheless one that (unlike a thermometer, which tells of but can have no fever) does not merely indicate but also incarnates time. Because it is not a datum of the flesh and much less of the spirit, a body is that body in whose grip the human being is a created being, even possibly in the sense of an automaton, as delightfully conceived by Descartes or, though somewhat unexpectedly, as dreaded by Pascal. Admittedly, because it is made of flesh and blood the body can simulate life. It dissimulates and hides itself as much from itself as from God. Downsized to a mere technique of flesh and blood, it worships no God lest it should worship and enshrine false gods. No wonder, for biblical religion, flesh and blood cannot reveal God. Nor is the body sacralized; it is simply indicative of one's mode of being in the world. This world is precisely a world in which God cannot be taken for granted, unless the world should be robbed of its worldhood (i.e., of its secularity). It is no wonder either that the incarnation consists, not in the enshrining of the word, but in its worlding, its secularization. Through the Christ-event, the eternal breaks into the secular as it does into time, into that which, lasting once and for all, as with all flesh, is an instance of eternity—an occasion to hallow the everlasting, to redeem time.

It is not that now flesh and blood can somehow point to God. No body can point to God any more than language can point beyond itself, much less to God as though to some bird's-eye view. God is no name for any bird's-eye view of all that is. Biblical religion precisely recants this kind of God. It holds that God is language. The God that speaks is no God that is God beyond time, beyond language. Being at an equal distance from all that is, once and for all or, for that matter, time and again, God breaks forth into time. In the words of Gregory of Nyssa, "the Timeless steps into time" even as the word becomes flesh and is worlded. It is worlded, that is, "secularized," insofar as in this worlding of the word, the world is not grasped in terms of worldliness, worthy of nothing but contempt, but is grasped in terms of the *saeculum* and is therefore honored as the arena of faith. The eternal happens through the secular, and accordingly, so long as no God is beyond the God that speaks but a God through whose word we are spoken for, neither flesh nor blood need any longer point beyond time, beyond language, whether to God or to no God.

No body takes God for granted. Affirming that no God is God, the body denies that God is no God. It is not the body but man and woman who, so far as they are expressive of its verbal condition, are created in the image of God. They are, however, created in the image of an imageless God, of a God that speaks, a God to whom, therefore, the biblical tradition attributes no sex. Like the body, this tradition does not take God for granted, either, and to that extent it is no more theistic or atheistic than it is sexist.

This non-theism of the body is the great discovery of a tradition for which the mythologem of the God that dies and is born again gives way to the notion of a God whose word becomes flesh. The arrogant height of atheism is reached, not by the death of God or by sheer stubborn unbelief, but by self-righteousness and the injustice it revels in, by sin and dying of life rather than living up to death yet without living it down. Salvation deals not with the way we die and what follows but with the way we live. It does not lie in the past but points to our future. Nor does a tomb seal it. The tomb is empty. Life is, through the Risen One, no longer centered on gods that die and rise again. Much less does the God of Jesus die with him—though not because the God of Israel cannot die (as Jesus's opponents would think), but because this God is the wholly other God.

This God is the very God in whose image we are created and, for this reason, are not owned by God let alone by ourselves, any more than a daughter is owned by her mother, or a son is owned by his father, or for that matter Isaac by Abraham and Jesus even by his Father in heaven. But just as Isaac is liberated from Abraham's possessive God, so is Jesus. There comes a time when the bond must be broken if the mutual otherness on which it rests has turned into mutual bondage. It is a bondage to which, on the one hand, Jesus no less than Isaac seems to consent out of sheer faithfulness; and a bondage about which, on the other hand, they reason as they must unless, complying with their sacrifice, they become suspect of being innocent of the guilt they incur.[7] "But where is the lamb for the burnt offering?" asks Isaac, still trusting his father's good faith[8] even as Jesus still trusts his God when he cries out to him, "Why hast thou forsaken me?"[9]

Consciously or unconsciously, both Isaac and Jesus break a bond. And each time a new covenant is so to speak "cut" with God (as the Hebrew language would put it), it symbolizes a shift of the relation between the divine and the human from mutual bondage to mutual otherness. No more than in the end Abraham's God accepts the sacrifice of Isaac does God accept the sacrifice of Jesus. Where is the lamb? asks Isaac of his father, who finally settles for a ram. Where is the Lamb of God that takes away the sins of the world, when a scapegoat is crucified and in extreme dereliction Jesus himself is forsaken by God?

Indeed, the scene unfolds as if, instead of being reasoned with, God needed to be appeased and Jesus, who reasons with God, is not heard and, forsaken by God, is made to "bear sin because of him."[10] He must die. His death is not only turned into a ritual sacrifice of atonement but is also ordained by God. But then what kind of God is it that would countenance, on the part of a people gone astray, what he clearly rejected on the part of Abraham, the father of faith? Abraham, rebuffed, is raised to fatherhood. Jesus is raised to humanhood: he who must die is no God. Much less is Jesus a God that cannot assume his humanity unless he goes through the bitter end of it. He must die as would a man, a man who is forsaken by, or has forsaken all claims to, God: there is no God in contrast to whom God is God. And Jesus is indeed forsaken so long as we go on clinging—and God knows we do keep on clinging—to the sacrificial apparatus of religion, an apparatus meant to be voided once and for all and yet has been and is voided again and again ever since the Garden of Eden had no sacred precinct and until the New Jerusalem has no room for a temple. Isaac is returned to Abraham, who until then was actually but a father according to the flesh. On Easter morning, Jesus is returned to his people, to those for whom God is not God for the dead but for the living.

The God who "becomes man" does not become some "little Jesus." If Jesus himself, insofar as he is the Christ, has any claim, this claim precisely consists of having of the God who "becomes man" neither a monopoly nor exclusive possession.[11] Jesus is not some superlative name for God but the common name of a God for every human being concerned with being human. Indeed, "there is no other name under heaven given among men by which we must be saved";[12] we have it in common and yet through it we are distinguished from one another. So common is this name that, in order to name God, we need no longer look for it beyond language (as did the builders of the Tower of Babel). We need look for no other name. Standing for God's radical otherness, it so radicalizes God that God's name is at one and the same time both secularized and hallowed. Abraham's children according to the flesh or, for that matter, Israel's very election may well continue to be a testimony to the God who saves and wears a different name depending on which side of the fence we stand. And yet the just and the wicked, on whom the sun continues to shine, are no less a testimony to the God who, though he saves, is no less a God that rules and ushers us through the thick and thin of nature or shepherds us through the ups and downs of history.

The God of the Bible is a God who feels and contends for us. Instead, we make God out to be a Savior, not to say a lifesaver. The God of grace is God freely available: we make of God a God of "grace and favours," like those granted by the princes of this world. Failing to be able to save the world, which God loves so much,[13] we seek, instead of changing it, to be saved from it and sanction by the same token the principle of a dual society. Abrasive as Karl Kautsky's judgment was, it was not entirely unmerited, and it still bears pondering. He writes, "Christianity became victorious only after it had been transformed into its opposite; not the proletariat was victorious in Christianity but the exploiters who monopolized the clergy. Christianity became victorious not as a destructive force, but as a conserving power, as a new reinforcement of exploitation and oppression."[14] Kautsky may well have been carried away. Even in eliminating a share of excess from this judgment, it still compels us to grant him that, at least on a strictly religious level, things are not much different today.[15]

Consider the incarnation: it has been so construed as to hark back to the exodus from Egypt rather than to the creation. Historically, the exodus took place before anything was written about the creation. But that is precisely no reason for Israel to highjack its liberator. God is no domestic God. Israel's redeemer is no less the maker of all that is, or else the ultimate end of all this, the eschatic fulfillment of time, would be swallowed by history, even though this history be that of the chosen people. Israel owes its liberation obviously not to some privilege wrested from God but only to God's grace, so gratuitously granted to it as never to be taken for granted. And this grace, whether it fulfills history or perfects nature, does neither without being iconoclastic of both.

Lest Israel should forget this iconoclastic edge of its own understanding of God, it is appropriately reminded that creation comes before its liberation and that the God who shepherds the Israelites out of Egypt not only was but is and remains the maker of all that is. Israel's election notwithstanding, salvation need not blunt the iconoclastic edge of the creative word. Nor is it necessary, by turning the incarnation into a blueprint of salvation, to numb its equally iconoclastic edge. No less an idol is the God whose worship should serve only to warrant and be warranted by privileges oddly in need of protection against the future. Privileges can neither save nor be saved, much less against the future. In the desert, no sooner was the manna saved for tomorrow than it went bad. Likewise, no sooner do we swerve from the incarnation and the worlding of the word it implies, regardless of whom God's sun continues to shine on, than salvation tips into a prudential ideology, consisting of sorting out those who believe from those who do not believe.

To say the least, this kind of ideology goes against the grain of Jesus's radical questioning of a tradition for which salvation is reduced to the commemoration of a cultural particularism. He proclaims the kingdom of God, and we manage to muffle its essentially eschatological dimension by couching it in terms of a religious particularism pegged on nothing less than a conundrum: we are not worthy of salvation, but others, at worst equally unworthy of it, are excluded from it. Yet Paul had warned against such a deviation. By declaring that through the Christ, as metaphoric hub of the divine and the human and site of the word made flesh, "there is neither Jew nor Greek, slave nor free, man nor woman,"[16] Paul puts into question the narrowing of the metaphor of salvation to its story.

The Christ does not overshadow Jesus the Jewish teacher. Much less does Jesus need to overshadow the christic metaphor of the divine and the human of which he is but the emblem. A story is always particular; it thinks for us. A symbol is universal, if only because it is not even a purely natural phenomenon. Yet in its ultimate contingency, it gives mouth to our body—to the embodiment of language, to "dogma," provided that this term is restored to its original liturgically accredited intention and does not refer to its present, discredited, meaning. And restored to the ecstasy of the mind and the basic experience of embodied life rather than to their control. Undoubtedly, those who initially tackled the metaphor of the Christ in terms of a twofold nature were not unaware of Paul's warning. They knew—as James Joyce, here unequaled by any theologian, will make plain—that a Jew who was Greek was not a chimaera, but that, Jew and Greek, these two were even more compatible than were any other two who were merely complementary to one another.

Unfortunately, the dogma that was subsequently developed so idealized both the divine and the human as to tie them down to one another in a way that Jesus himself would have rebuked and Paul denounces when he points out that we do not know the Christ by the flesh. Paul urges us to view all things through the eyes of faith alone, and to realize likewise that in Christ there is no God or "man," either, as even Calvin suggests.[17] What else can one recognize God by, or for that matter the human, if not by what each of them is not, as Jesus himself implies when he states that whoever sees him sees God?[18] No God is God that can be turned into an idol, as anyone should have known who, deifying Jesus, defies his solidarity with both our human condition and his God.

In the parable of the Last Judgment, there are those who help the hungry or thirsty and welcome strangers, and those who do not; the former are greeted into the Lord's company, and yet they were no more aware of actually helping or receiving the Lord than were the latter, who did not and are rejected.[19] Having not ever seen God, none of them had in fact acted in the name of God. But has anyone ever seen God? And whose fault is it? Certainly not God's—at least for Jesus, who hastens to exonerate God. Faced with the man blind from birth, "[Jesus's] disciples . . . put to him the question: Rabbi, who sinned, this man or his parents, that he was born blind?" Jesus replies: "It is not that he or his parents were sinful; but so that the works of God should be manifested in him." Far from the disciples, indeed, was any idea of setting a trap for Jesus. But it is nevertheless on them that a trap closes. It is they who have "their mouths and their tongues confused." Did they not expect Jesus to cite that very passage from Exodus where Moses resists God under the pretext of having no facility with language? But Moses hears himself being told: "Who has made man's mouth? and who makes him dumb or deaf, seeing or blind? Is it not I, the Eternal?"[20]

God hangs on our lips. Tough for the disciples! Could it be that they understand Jesus no better than the scribes and Pharisees who now, it seems, are not sure that they understand Moses, either? At any rate, Jesus is telling all of them that the work of God manifests itself even in the person whose sight is blind through no fault of his or whose mouth draws tight like shutters on her body instead of rehearsing it again and again in the praise of the Lord. Admittedly, she cannot perhaps speak about God. But she can speak of God, since God can only be spoken of with words that are not per se meant for speaking of God. God has no etymology. God takes root in words, which have no roots. Rather than on nature (physicalism) or on the mystical (spiritualism), God hangs on language, on a word that bodies forth, by grace enfranchised. That this can happen is what is precisely attested through that event in which, indeed, the Christ need not have been Jesus and which, therefore, happens once and for all—wherever the word is worlded, whether in relation to God or in our relation with others, or in reaction to a thing of beauty, or in our quest for truth, or in our consciousness of finitude, or again in confronting suffering and death. It happens wherever being human is pending and, ever on sufferance, hope is within the reach of any human being.

"God becomes man." No other bridging of words was ever achieved in a more supreme abridgment of language, and so sublime—but that was long ago. And yet the formula is all the more striking today; it need no longer be taken literally—if it ever was. Or else it would lack credibility, though no fault lies in the formula. The fault lies in its two extremities: "God" and "man." Today "God" may even be a "she," but she does not become woman. The "myth" has become so tough-skinned that one could indifferently say either that it is nothing but a myth or that it no longer is a myth. And yet aside from its mythic ring, the bridging of "God" and "man" does have something to do with christology, with the person and work of Jesus as the Christ, that is, with the worlding of the word and the humanizing of God, not to speak of the human being.

Still, one is faced with the question *"Cur Deus homo?"* Why does God become "man"? It is a question that arises if not in the wake of, at least in keeping with, another: "Why is there something rather than nothing?" Probably they are one and the same question. How could one be astonished that anything is if one is not capable of love? Wonder and love form a pair. Just as astonishment occurs when the given is turned into a gift, or wonder turns the world into wonderland, so love turns the self into an other. There is no love, and no astonishment either, where there is no possibility for otherness and where without otherness there is no possibility of solidarity. If anything is, then it can be transfigured, even as the word can become flesh—and salvation consists in changing the world rather than in changing worlds.

An insidious and equally absurd question, however, immediately comes to mind. Could it be that christology, like technology, not to mention science, could arise only in the West? Or conversely could it be that, and again like science and technology, it is time for christology to be emancipated from strictly Western patterns of thought? Like it or not, at the very least, christology needs to be revisited if only because, in the wake of such questioning, is brought to light the extent to which traditional sacrificial christology has deviated from the eschatism of the word become flesh. In this christology, the notion of a God, who loves the world so much that, making it the gift of his Son, he makes it his utopia, gives way to a Son who must, indeed, die to save us, poor sinners, though he meant to change the world. He wanted justice. He will instead draw to himself only those who are satisfied with another solution—with charity—and accordingly, for want of justice, are satisfied with the makeshift of the least evil, with law and order. Instead of highlighting the worlding of the word, christology gives way to a make-do christological centralism. It gives way to an eyewash christology jeopardized in the long run by sexism, by racism, and by the imperialism of a dogmatic monopolistic orthodoxy. Instead of the New Testament's assertion that salvation is through the christic event made available to Jew and Greek alike, now we are told there is no salvation outside the church. And so, together with salvation, God becomes the monopoly of a church oblivious of the fact that Israel had already been rebuked by the prophets for pretending to have a similar monopoly on God even though it was God who chose Israel and not the other way around.[21]

The church can therefore claim no monopoly on christology unless it insists on barring either the Jew or the Greek from the "benefits" of that very Christ through whom no line can be drawn between Jew and Greek, let alone between the church and the world. Ontotheism, as reprehensible as otherwise it could be held to be, had at least understood that its logocentrism was only the price of its inclusiveness. But, restricted to the West by this same inclusiveness, ontotheism was driven to mistake the pleromatic[22] experience of worlding the word for a totalitarian if universalistic hegemony exerted by the church at the expense of the word—as the reformers will keep reminding us. This ontotheism of the West and its imperialism go hand in hand. But each is in fact deluded by the other. When they falter, it will not be because their hieratically domineering stance will suddenly make them look superannuated. It will be because, though they still pretended to come under the purview of the incarnation, they actually distorted its eschatic dimension; they disqualified themselves.

In the light of the incarnation, the basic experience of life is not designed to be in accord with some unifying principle whether of totality or of universality; it is pegged on the fullness of time, when God is all in all and there is no temple in the New Jerusalem. It is a principle of social and political iconoclasm, of cultural and religious dissent. "The eschatological character of Christian existence," as Bultmann puts it, "is never a datum of this world, but the permanent limitation of one's being-in-the-world." But then, he adds, "Christian existence is what it is only when it does not cease from tackling its limits,"[23] from pushing them back. It does this by simply keeping from thwarting the worlding of the word and by allowing the secular to come into its own—despite the sacralizing temptation to which it is exposed and may succumb in other respects because of inherited conceptual as well as social structures from which it is never perfectly enough enfranchised. For instance, viewing, with Anne Fremantle, the medieval period as the "age of belief," of faith, may not be wholly inappropriate.[24] It would be grievously misleading if we should overlook the fact that this period was also pregnant with the autonomy of the secular and led to its amplification through the Reformation. Across the ages, it is therefore safe to claim that—with or without ecclesiastic blessing—Christian existence, as attested to by the rising tide of the secular, does not cease from enlarging its horizon by withstanding and otherwise by withholding from the dogmatism of the culture it has itself generated.

That dogmatism of the West, like its imperialism, does not stem directly from christology; it stems from metaphysical presuppositions of a theology that is subsequently so carried away by the christological centralism to which it will surrender that it deflects its intellectual commitment to the Christ-event, and that any concomitant, independent if not autonomous, anthropology is aborted.[25] It is as if, the New Testament notwithstanding, there could be no concept of the human being except against the background of an ineluctably saving God. But, as Bultmann points out, already in the New Testament, "the revealer appears not as *man-in-general*, i.e. not simply as a bearer of human *nature*, but as *a definite human being in history:* Jesus of Nazareth. His humanity is genuine humanity: 'the word became flesh.'" Accordingly, Bultmann adds, the Gospel of John "has no theory about the pre-existent one's miraculous manner of entry into the world nor about the manner of his union with the man Jesus."[26] In the New Testament, Herbert Braun points out, christology is what varies, while anthropology is what does not. One is not surprised if, subsequently, from one century to another, "every later picture of Jesus . . . is in fact . . . but a picture of what in the New Testament is already a picture."[27]

Nevertheless, whatever anthropology there is, it is developed under the protection of a christology that, instead of being focalized by a dialectic of word and deed, is itself significantly mortgaged by a devious metaphysics of being (and non-being). This subordination of anthropology does not ebb. It even continues with Barth or Bonhoeffer and, oddly yet not quite unexpectedly, with some chroniclers of the death of God, for whom Jesus looms in our orphaned memory as the pattern of the man for others. And yet a man not like others?

Most sensitive, the question deals with the identification of the Christ of faith and the historical Jesus. It deals, I should rather say, with the way in which they are deferred to each other, neither being able to assert itself without asserting the other. And yet the Christ of faith is one thing; the Jesus of history and his own faith, his religion, is another. Should even, as Ernst Bloch claims, Jesus's own demonstration of love for God be and remain unequaled throughout the history of religion, "his humanity is [and, Bultmann keeps on contending, remains] genuine humanity."[28] No particular "bearer of human nature," in no way does Jesus "appear as man-in-general but as a definite human being in history: Jesus of Nazareth."[29] Christology need neither eclipse nor be eclipsed by anthropology. Labeled a man for others or man for his fellow men, Jesus tends, some critics aver, to look like he has just survived the demise of God; or, what would amount to the same, he looks like he was rescued from the tentacles of a henceforth improbable surrogate divinity, thanks, supposedly, to the transition from a vertical to a horizontal christology—horizontal and yet no less truncated, given the fact that such a christology is then exclusively pegged on the character of human beings largely reduced to their social functions and more or less defrauded of their other qualities.

Christ is no God written in small caps. Nor is he "man" written in capital letters. At the core whether of the historical Jesus or of the Christ of faith lies the far more significant question of the proclaimer becoming the proclaimed,[30] that is, the believer's relation through a Christ that is neither God nor "man" to the "godhood" of God and its concomitant notion of the worldhood of the world. Feuerbach notwithstanding, theology is not so much anthropology as it is christology, pegged as it is, not on some dialect of faith, but on worlding a word become flesh and lying not so much beyond as—not unlike the self between subject and object—between all presumed opposition of the religious and the secular.

In fact, the real problem is not linked with the substitution of a horizontal christology for a vertical one. The horizontal is already implicit in the vertical, for a simple reason. A sacrificial christology, the vertical revolves around a Christ who dies for our sins. Appearances to the contrary, the horizontal itself ends up falling back on a mere surrogate of the classic otherworldly mystique of salvation. Jesus, no savior from on high, still is a savior of sorts. Cut-rate or not, salvation baffles the incarnation. At that cost, even Hans Urs von Balthasar demurs. Is he losing his bearings? He claims that "there is no question of applying to Christ a definition which would distinguish him as man essentially for other men, setting him apart for instance as 'man for his fellow men.'" But immediately he lets the cat out of the bag. "Such an account," he states, "of what Christ and other men are respectively only brings out the specifically social, horizontal function of nature, prudently omitting its relation to God."[31] Balthasar is falling between two stools. For him, Jesus, no "man-in-general," is not "the man from Nazareth," not a man *tout court*, either. Nor is Jesus, however, one for whom vertical and horizontal, religious and secular, and wording God and worlding the word belong together. Balthasar restricts the incarnation to salvation, even as the cosmic to the mystical.

If there is a problem, it must lie elsewhere—in the fact that, in keeping with the eschatic logic of the incarnation, christology, call it horizontal then if you will, is nevertheless bound up with the recovery of the secular as the sole condition for the worldhood of the world, even as it is equally bound up with being human as the sole condition for the recovery of the human being. It calls for a faith that, to the extent it is committed to God, is also involved with the world and, rather than holding it in contempt, honors it as the theater of God's glory, even though on today's show is still enacted a scene about an unlikely shepherd looking for a lost sheep.

Faith is not an enclosure sheltered from the age or from the world. It is not celebrated in a church choir or a chancel (*chœur*) but at the heart (*cœur*) of the world, through its very secularity. And yet the secular, generated however theoretically by the church, is more often than not passed over or betrayed rather than reclaimed and put into practice. The reason is simple enough. Christian faith is articulated through a christology that is only one focus—the other being anthropology—of an ellipse itself governed by a theology still haunted by ontotheism, by the supernatural, by the other world. It matters little in that case that christology is vertical or horizontal—it is centripetal, and expectedly so. The social body is itself modeled on the body of Christ. Anthropology remains under the firm protection of a christology acting as vanguard of a total-God theology.[32] In contrast to this kind of approach, I have proposed elsewhere that if both the divine and the human are in the hands of language and if both of them hang on the worlding of the word, in other words if Christ is the word made flesh, then christology alone can have primacy over theology properly speaking, as does language over being, whether divine or human. Christology, that is to say, language, is then that ellipse of which the foci are God and the human. Even as language, so the Christ is also the measure of God and the human.

Christ—Neither God Nor Man

Consider Calvin. The whole range of his thought is ordered to the principle of the inner witness of the Holy Spirit, that is to say to the phenomenality of the word, which he tackles by comparing the knowledge of God and the knowledge of one's self. But as to which of them comes before the other,[33] he does not hesitate and, immediately, observes that this is a moot question. More important for him is the fact that, proceeding from as well as through the knowledge of Christ, they hang on it. His point is well taken. More straightforward in this respect than Luther, Calvin does not restrict christology to the theme of salvation. Restoring its eschatic edge—the glorification and the honor of God—he recasts it as a process of worlding the word. Descriptively put, he replaces a centripetal christology with a centrifugal one. And in the wake of this christological shift, he paves the way for a new understanding of the church. Instead of evoking a hard core of initiates or, alternately, a bleeding heart no less intent on keeping the world at a distance albeit under its spell, the church is not viewed as some sluice or flood chamber between this world and the next but is likened to the leaven in the dough it makes rise. Church and world are meshed together. If the former must still account for the latter, this is only because the latter is actually the instrument of the former.

In the Middle Ages, religion was in charge of the secular, fostering it; now it must itself come of age through the secular, should this entail its own secularization. To know the Christ is to know his benefits (Melanchthon). Life in the spirit is life in the world, if the world must at all be hallowed and changed instead of being held in contempt. Ironically, whether on a religious or a cultural level, the assessment of such a switch—and, for its succinctness, the most pertinently couched in christological terms[34]—we owe to Pascal's acuity. He writes, "The knowledge of God without that of man's misery causes pride. The knowledge of man's misery without that of God causes despair. The knowledge of Jesus Christ constitutes the middle course, because in Him we find both God and our misery."[35] We find the sign of the gratuitousness not only of God but of the incarnation itself: Jesus is but the witness of it. Instead of referring us to himself, he defers us to ourselves when he defers us to God, just as he defers us to God when he defers us to ourselves. "The incarnation shows man the greatness of his misery by the greatness of the remedy which he required."[36]

It is no surprise if Feuerbach, too, naturally comes to mind here. He reduced theology to mere anthropology. He could have been better inspired had he instead viewed anthropology as the conditioning of theology. He would have realized that, in the myth of the incarnation, the God that "becomes man" does not take him hostage. God is released from us even as we are released from God. The incarnation not only warns us against turning God into an idol; it also shows us the futility of it all if faith means being enfranchised from the need to turn God into an idol. What stands in opposition to theonomy is not human autonomy. It is heteronomy, which, gnawing at one and corroding the other, corrupts them both, pitting one against the other.

A poor father was Abraham, were he but our father according to the flesh, as Jesus points out. The Jews who claim Abraham for a father are not and will not be forsaken by God. For descendants of Abraham, such a God cannot and does not die. This is a God who saves and therefore need not, in contrast to pagan gods, die and be born again. But then he could be an idol and, if so, who could tell the difference between God and the idol? Words are ambiguous. Language is ambivalent: an idol lurks behind God; or else, the God that dies is an idol, while the idol is a God that cannot die and yet is only survived by a fossilized language. We become orphans of a God that cannot die and yet is no longer the Living One, the God of Abraham, and of Isaac, and of Jacob, as Jesus points out to his fellow Jews when he cries out, "My God, why hast thou forsaken me?" Death alienates us from ourselves as well as from God—from worlding the word through which we are spoken for.

For biblical religion, salvation has clearly nothing to do with dying and rising gods or, for that matter, with gods that cannot die or would die only by proxy. When Paul says that "the Lord of glory has been crucified,"[37] it is not, Calvin suggests, that he has suffered anything in his divinity, "but that Jesus Christ, who suffered that ignominious death in the flesh, himself was the Lord of glory."[38] Making God into an idol that does not die is bad enough. Making Jesus into a God that dies and in the process defrauds the man Jesus of his death is even worse. Jesus neither substitutes himself for a God that dies, nor does he substitute himself for the Jews' idol that does not die. Lest Calvin's point still need clarification, we have only to remember that he "rejects categorically the ubiquity of the body of Christ" and that he does so "for the same reasons that make him reject every attempt at the deification of man"—including, François Wendel adds, even that "of the person of Jesus Christ."[39]

Historically speaking, however, although Jesus is divinized and stands for a God that dies and rises again, he is nevertheless the Son of God; as the Christ of God, he is Son to a God who cannot and does not die. Clearly, consistently, even the trinitarian tradition of the church has always asserted that only God the Son and not God the Father dies on the cross. In contrast to the logic of the word made flesh, however, it drives a wedge between God and the world, between transcendence and immanence. They are no longer in the hands of language. And Christianity, instead of keeping with the biblical tradition and being a religion of the word, both is and is not a religion of salvation, concerned with saving the soul in some other world rather than tipping the human being into being human and changing this world.

Could it be that through the personification of the Messiah, through the deification of Christ, a concession was made to the paganism of soteric religions? By letting the gratuitousness of God's grace give way to barter (between God and the devil for our ransom), could it be that the God of Abraham was filtered out, just as, in the Christian iconography, the synagogue was to appear blindfolded to the benefit of a church, clear-sighted yet no less slighted with blinders of its own devising? Was Alfred Loisy right? Jesus, he says, came proclaiming the kingdom of God, and we got the church, did we not?[40] The church keeps thinking of natural "man" as sinful, of the past as something to repent, and, thinking backward, keeps its eyes on the rearview mirror. The church is concerned with screening off Christianity from assorted Jews and sundry "heretics" or would-be unbelievers, not to mention believers of another persuasion. Unlike believers, including its own, that are essentially migrant, the God of the church is no different from gods that do not migrate, except at the point of bayonets. By contrast, the God of Jesus does not stay put but looks forward and "becomes man." This is so much so that "Christ's divinity is best seen in looking at his humanity."[41] And human beings are being human to the extent that they stand at an equal distance from God or that God is equally near to all. Whether Messiah or Christ, "[t]he term does not refer to the nature of a person but to a function to be performed by someone (whether human or divine) in the course of God's saving and judging action."[42]

"The heavens are telling the glory of God, the firmament proclaims the work of his hands. Day to day pours forth speech, night to night declares knowledge." But, the psalmist adds, "There is no speech, there are no words, their voice is not heard"[43]—except by those gifted with speech, with language. It is to Adam that God says "thou." Whoever is addressed as "thou" is not only spoken to but spoken for. Through language the human being is committed to being human.

No one speaks who is not spoken for. No one speaks who does not trust, and trusting God, like trusting others, amounts to neither more nor less than worlding the word. A treasury of words, language is the treasury of faith, its earthen and its heavenly vessel at once. It scans faith and even the timing of it, even though faith, insofar as it is language, is always on time with the word.

Faith, however, is not to be reduced to the language of faith. From the first to the second Adam, the language of faith is not the same. Faith does not cancel another faith. If it did, it would cancel itself. The first Adam is not canceled by the second. Like being human, faith happens once and for all, even as, encompassing past and future, time happens once and for all. Or else there would be a time when time was not. There would be a time before the word becomes flesh, when the word was not. But the word, having no space, has no past. It was with God and even is God, says the prologue of John's Gospel.

The incarnation does not mark some midpoint of a linear time, between creation and pleroma, between a beginning and an end. It is, instead, time that is the milieu of the incarnation, even as it is the milieu of God's everlasting reign, through which the eternal happens once and for all. Otherwise, God would have a past and become a God of ancestors. Rather than being human first, Adam would merely be the first human being, a product of nature or some avatar of history. Similarly, it is therefore said of Jesus, the second Adam, that he was conceived by the Holy Spirit and born of a virgin.

Whatever may have been the pertinence—it is not negligible—of traditional christological patterns, they cease to achieve their aim, and they are transformed into mausoleums of religion, when they forget that this religion is not a religion of nature or even of salvation but a religion of the word, an iconoclastic religion constantly in need of overcoming itself. It will never rest in any particular language of faith, lest language, instead of obliterating itself, should stiffen into a formula even while the word is being worlded. And Christ Jesus becomes a formula, even screening us off from faith and standing in its way, forgetting that nature, like history, cannot tell the glory of God unless it keeps from personifying God or divinizing a man. The word become flesh is not a soteriological mythologem. And the Christ is not a datum even of faith but its realization, as Paul suggests when he writes, "For me, to live is Christ."[44] It is to be in the hands of language, an instrument of the worlding of the word.

Against this background, a theory of the two natures of Christ was developed nevertheless—and drafted by committees that must have been fearful for us humans. They must have feared that we would puff ourselves up inordinately and become swollen with pride, with hubris—and that that hubris had to be bridled. Or was there some reason to fear for God? Did they fear that God was already superfluous?

It is true that, contrary to the virtue of the Greeks, faith is not a "happy medium" between two extremes, between belief and unbelief. There is no middle course between sin and grace. *Simul justus ac peccator,* at once justified and sinful, Luther keeps repeating about each of us. The believer, Pascal points out in a slightly different mood, is a righteous person who believes himself to be a sinner, while the sinner believes himself to be righteous.

Even more than a fear either for God or for us humans must have been the fear of lacking faith—unless being bereft of mystery and deprived of miracles was thought to mean that one only belonged together with people of little faith. True also, despite a good many prevailing ideas on the humility of the religious animal, we did not wait for the mirages of science and technology before we started playing God. The sorcerer's apprentice did not wait for the soil of religion to become parched in order to get his act together; he had already done so when this soil was fertile. But, of course, it could simply be that, with "a God become man" in Christ, the latter's human nature had to be counterbalanced by a divine nature if only to keep to the biblical idea according to which only a God can still save us. Was it necessary, for all that, to defer salvation to a world beyond this world and yet so much the more anthropocentric that, in the course of centuries marked by Christianity, it will stand in sharp contrast with a universe less and less anthropocentric, as Pascal intimates, awed as he was by the eternal silence of an infinite space?

Infinite and no less sentenced to silence, space seems suddenly barred from telling the glory of God. It no longer points to God. No speech, no words, no voice is to be heard. An anthropotheocentric universe of discourse has collapsed. From representational, language becomes fictional. What frightens Pascal is not that the world has been dedivinized but that, being neither divine nor human, the order of things appears of a sudden as an order of words; and that nothing can account for the silence scattered out across the real except an equally fractured language conscious of its being fundamentally shorn of any unifying principle and yet sentenced forever to shore up its fragments. There are as many ways of structuring a language as there are words. There are as many ways of constructing and deconstructing the unspoken language of a silent universe as there are fragments in Pascal's discourse on his own method, which consists in writing down nothing with the would-be certainty of an eyewitness. Each fragment is a perception of a whole that remains unfinished, unfulfilled until the word becomes flesh and, though it dwells among us, is not heard. Pascal's fascination with the figure of Christ is the key to his way of thinking: neither linear nor circular, it rests on the primacy of language. A reed, he says, is what the human being is; but this is a thinking reed, which, because it can read and write, is an instrument of the worlding of the word and its timing. The silence of space may, possibly unlike time, be as indifferent to God as it is to humans: it calls for those that, having ears to hear and eyes to see, hear and see and yet believe. The feeling of having been dumped off an anthropotheocentric language that has disqualified itself was surely a shock. It was also for Pascal an eye-opener.

However brief a lifetime may be, it lasts forever if it lasts once and for all. Time throbs and has more affinities than space does with the notion of incarnation. A transfiguration of the temporal through the eternal, incarnation points to the overcoming of space by time. It points to the overcoming of silence by speech, of words by language.

Incarnation: a *kairos* of the word become flesh. Language: a *kairos* of the flesh becoming word, even through mere words. But then these are the very words by which metaphors are begotten, words also that, through their metaphorical spacing into a language, are deferred to one another in a symbolic and all the more real recovery of all that is real. And other. Without otherness, no language. No incarnation, either. Even as nothing comes before creation, so also does nothing come before incarnation or language, before that which happens once and for all—like time.

Time is of otherness. But this otherness lies not so much in things or beings in themselves as in their relation to one another; it consists not only in taking up a stance but also in going the distance between the self and the other, plotted in by language itself. Secularizing time, language calls for a secular understanding of the incarnation itself, which indeed lies in worlding the word, in extending it, from Israel to the nations, from the familiar mountain and its majestic grace to the silence of unheard-of spaces. Flat or curved, space confronts us with the necessity for this worlding to be retooled again and again. And rewording it is the only way of preventing the double-edged iconoclasm of the incarnation from turning against itself.

God does not become Christian; God "becomes man." Living off the Christ, no "man" comes before "man." Jesus himself rejects all anthropocentrism, as is for instance illustrated by his statement "Before Abraham was, I am." The question is no longer who comes before whom, and much less is it whether Christians supersede Jews, and so on. Pointless is the question of classifying humankind: the first will be the last and vice versa.

To the question "What is man?" the psalmist replies, "Almost a god,"[45] not the least embarrassed by the ambiguity of that "almost." It implies that the Jew is that human being whose being human guards him from taking himself for God—should this Jew even call himself Jesus, through whom "God becomes man," or, should the Jews as a whole have forgotten that no God is God if, for all the others, God should be but an idol. In the long run, it also credits Paul's contention that the world is swarming with gods, none of which is less superfluous than the other and, especially, that the worlding of the word, as designed by the very notion of incarnation, is brought to naught if it is deflected and hindered from desacralizing the world by secularizing faith, even God insofar as God is word. This word speaks to every human being that, speaking for itself, is spoken for being human. And Jesus is "to be made like his brethren in every respect."[46]

They made a God of him. Was Jesus not man enough? Or was the point of it all to impress everyone's unconscious with the very relativity of all theism, whether male or female, and sunk in polytheism and monotheism or, for that matter, in atheism?

Despite Paul's warnings, the myth of the incarnation, lurking into dogma, provides a pretext for extending and going further than Judaism. But Christianity cannot challenge Israel without challenging the nations: it overestimates Israel and underestimates the incarnation. The challenge has the look of an entrapment. The liturgical development of faith into dogma glosses over the very challenge that is supposed to be addressed to the nations. Trapped in dogma, Christianity becomes trapped in the world. But then this was a risk it had to take or else cease to lay claim to a specific role among the nations as well as to its attachment to Israel.

This is a quandary of which Abraham Geiger gives an idea, though not its full measure, when in a somewhat emphatic mood he writes, "If

[Christianity] gives up its pretensions, it ceases to be Christianity and reverts to a moment of Judaism which, once developed, tries to satisfy humanity's longing for salvation."[47] Whatever is meant by "humanity's longing for salvation," Judaism and Christianity are lumped together if this longing is to be quenched. It will be quenched by either of them: by Christianity, provided that it reverts to being a moment of Judaism, or by Judaism, if it develops this moment—and is itself possibly developed into a moment of Christianity? Instead, they both were trapped and not by each other: Christianity was to be by dogma as Judaism already was by the temple. In other words, each is similarly trapped by a world of its own doing. They can achieve their goal only if the religious tradition to which they equally subscribe is "deterritorialized" and the worlding of the word is in the power of *any* language, regardless of where this language is spoken, in Athens or in Jerusalem. Every language is a bridge or a gateway, not a sarcophagus.

Messiah, Christ, Son of God—these are not titles that Jesus claims for himself upon being baptized any more than he does upon his resurrection.[48] What Jesus claims is that, in spite of whom or what they say he is and even who or what Abraham was, he is neither more nor less than what he is. Unless he was Jesus, as they rightly though with a sneer supposed he merely was, he could not be "before" Abraham was. He has no one else to assume than himself. The word that, likewise, assumes the flesh does not assume the essence of humanity. It does not assume being human in general; it assumes a human being. Being human is what only a human being can be concerned with. Likewise, being the Christ is what Jesus can only be concerned with, and then not so much "because" he must be crucified or, even worse, "abandoned by God," but in spite of all that. Jesus need not die for our sins. He dies. And it is not because he dies but in spite of it that the Christ must be the Risen One. There is no causal necessity that is not dispelled by the resurrection. Jesus himself remains a contingent emblem of the Christ. He remains a Jew, and to that extent the Christ-event is a "moment" in the development of Judaism. For the same reason, Christianity cannot revert to Judaism without subverting it—without Israel being restored from a biological to the spiritual dimension of its descent from Abraham, the father of faith. Restored from *physis* to *nomos*—to Torah— Israel is restored to language. It is reinstated as instrument for worlding a language—be it its own—none of whose words is to be found in nature (as Derrida could say). And raised from the dead is only he who lies in the hands of language.

Not unlike Israel from one covenant to the other, through the Christ, even what Jesus is from birth to death is bracketed between virgin birth and resurrection. It is bracketed within language—even as between the Garden of Eden and the New Jerusalem or between the Tower of Babel and Pentecost, the world is in the biblical tradition bracketed until it is tipped into the kingdom of God, into that utopia of God's of which Christ, the word become flesh, is the key, the gateway.

"I am the door," says Jesus—not a tombstone rolled away for all to see. If Christ is the Risen One, it is not because of but in spite of the empty tomb. Listen again: "Because you have seen me, you have believed. Happy are those who have not seen me and have believed."[49] Happy are those who have not seen him as the Savior and yet have believed and have fed the hungry or sheltered the stranger within their gates. Happy are those for whom salvation happens on top of the bargain. The word become flesh heralds the kingdom and, conversely, the worlding of the word heralds the resurrection.

Extending God's covenant with the chosen people from Israel to the nations, the incarnation not only gathers all humankind into one body, it also represents its diversity.[50] What we all have in common is also what, in Christ, distinguishes us from one another—a language. Consisting in the worlding of the word, the incarnation aims not at the unification of religion so much as at the inauguration of a world secular enough to transcend the natural, mutual exclusivism typical of every religion, including even one that, claiming to be inclusive, remained oblivious of the secular. Severed from the secular, religion imposes itself. It is never immune from hiding a secular agenda. Conversely, the secular also imposes itself because it hides a religious agenda. No God is exposed because of the gap that yawns between them except a stopgap God. God is "exposed," but not imposed, only when the religious and the secular are brought together in worlding the word.[51] So also is the worldhood of the world exposed as that without which God is not God,[52] as that without which no God is God. Such is the world so loved by God as to be God's own utopia. It is a world in which Jesus personifies no God.

Jesus is a Jew. He does not take himself for God. Call him a Suffering Servant if we will, but he personifies this even less than he denounces the injustice of so-called social justice, a system of love that begins and ends with oneself. Call him the Savior if we will, but the salvation he ushers in consists rather in freeing us from our obsession with salvation (as Martin Luther intimates, without going, perhaps, as far as drawing out all the consequences).[53]

What the eternal is to the ephemeral, or time to the moment, the incarnation is to Jesus; it encompasses his earthly life, betokened by stories of a virgin birth and a resurrection—stories that are not meant to catch a glimpse of his life. The incarnation is not a moment but the milieu of his life. In claiming that he is "before Abraham was," Jesus neither cancels nor replaces Abraham. The incarnation is not a moment of history and not its midpoint, either. Abraham is betrayed by pretensions of those that descend from him according to the flesh. So also is Jesus, when in his name are soon to be condoned similar pretensions by those who, comforted by the pretext that spirituality has now replaced genealogy, go on repeating, "Lord! Lord!" They lessen the eschatological dimension of the incarnation to the dubious sacrificial story of a scapegoat for which the explanation is no different from Archibald MacLeish's about God: it is "reasons." Reasons serve to explain everything—even Auschwitz. Reason cannot. Neither can faith, unless it is "God is reasons," unless in the name of the Christ some are saved and others are not, as a selective christology would still have it.

Increasingly confronted with other religions as well as with its own biblical sources, such a christology can no longer be indulged, except at the price of its object. Today's mood recoils from funding any basic life experience with the idea of a death by proxy, be it that of Jesus. Sinfulness notwithstanding, in these days of lagging biblical culture such an idea is even offensive, especially after Auschwitz and the substitutionary ideology that led to it, regardless of whether that ideology was a drifting parody, a despicable distortion of the very finality of such a christology.[54] What this christology overlooked is the point made by Paul when, realizing that the cross is a stumbling block for Jews and folly for Greeks, he intimates that, through the Christ, even this cleavage is brought to an end.[55] It makes sense only from a historicist point of view. Instead of the miracles Jews call for and the wisdom Greeks look for or religious aspirations for which, symbolically, miracles and wisdom stand for, Paul puts forward the cross. No symbol for anything noble, much less for the nobility of death, and even turned into a farce, it nevertheless catches the culturally sensitive imagination of a religious migrant such as Paul. The cross no doubt stands above all as the most incredible of all possible religious symbols. But it opens the door to a radical reconfiguration of the religious question, centering it on the worlding of the word as space of creation and fulfillment.

A dead end for those sentenced to it, the cross is the anti-symbol par excellence of salvation, whether through divine power or through human reason. Bereft both of power and wisdom, it brings to an end our obsession with this or that mode of being, whether Greek or Jewish. The most unnatural of all symbols, it goes against the grain of religion. Traditional religious symbols are rooted in nature. So paradoxical a symbol of faith, indeed, could only hang on a cross. It does not magnify, nor does it detract from a natural phenomenon. No river crosses another river. Likewise, no religion crosses another. Neither do the vertical and the horizontal cross each other, except through language. The same applies to the natural and the historical, to transcendence and immanence, to the divine and the human. Or to Good Friday and Easter. The incarnation not only stands for the word that heals, it also stands for the worlding of the word—not only for the New Being, but also for the New Creation. As a moment of Judaism, it also stands for religion overcoming itself or, for that matter, crossing itself out.

No God is God. Whatever name God is known by, it is crossed out, even be it that of Jesus—the man from Nazareth, "the stone rejected by the builders which becomes the chief cornerstone," whom, because of self-authenticating pretensions, "you have crucified, and whom God has raised from the dead."[56] Even as Jesus is rooted in and yet is "crossed" out of Israel, so also does faith cross itself out through the worlding of the word in which it is at stake. This is a faith that, Bultmann writes, so far as it is eschatic existence, rests on "the fact that Jesus as the 'Word' (that became flesh) has nothing with which to identify himself: it is the man, Jesus of Nazareth, through whom God comes to us, without Jesus being able to prove his authenticity as the Son of God."[57] "If it does not lead to action, it is in itself a dead thing."[58] Faith lies in its performance, and to the degree that it says what it does and does what it says, it needs no safety net.

I borrow from Michel Henry his dazzling rendering of John 8:58: *"Avant Abraham, moi, la vie"* (Before Abraham, me, a life). The phrase is so aptly rendered that, like an endoscopy, it exposes the heart and matter of the incarnation: missing is *a* verb—though not *the* verb, the worlding of the word to which it points. The incarnation calls for no verb, no wording that would objectify its reality. It does not consist in objectifying the reality of a God of whom one would then wish to say that God is here or that God is there.

Verbum caro: it is by its worlding that one recognizes the word, as it is by the flesh that one recognizes the spirit. An objectified God would be a God without an object, more superfluous than gratuitous, a God that dies—and relieves us from the injustice committed in God's name. A God, used as a crutch, is a God who, instead of dwelling in our flesh, obsesses us with our salvation. Unlike a father or a mother for their child, such a God makes no room for us. Only the God that dwells in our flesh can make room for us. So does the word that becomes flesh dwell in a language and yet has no language of its own.[59]

God—being no god—belongs to no given religious language, and the incarnation is no parochializing of the word become flesh.

Fictions of Faith

3

> They are rid of the Christian God and now believe all the more firmly that they must cling to Christian morality.
>
> By searching out origins, one becomes a crab. The historian looks backward; eventually he also believes backward.
>
> —Nietzsche, *Twilight of the Idols*

No parochializing of the word become flesh, language comes into its own nowhere but through worlding the word, resolving faith into—yet without dissolving—the world. The real, a fiction of language, is a fiction of faith.

Faith is a passion. For Kierkegaard, this passion is a passion for words, for the word, even for worlding the word. So evident is this that he cannot think of a single name under which all its flow might be collected in writing. He underwrites what he writes under a pseudonym. No name can shelter him from being called to account for what he underwrites. Kierkegaard is unique—in other people's eyes. Crashing his life as others crash a party, he finds it to be an eye-opener: there is no greater simulator of itself than the self. Prompted to deceive itself and caught at its own game, it can but reveal itself. It is scattered.

An Ethic of the Unprecedented

Scattered through a bundle of words, the self is hardly collectible in any one vocable, or under a name. Names are separators. They personify. Or they impersonate. Yet in spite—if not because—of the much debased "they," "*they* call me" (*on m'appelle*) rings truer than the more classic and self-advertising "my name is." It is mine only because it was given me, as is made plain even by the apparently unilateral French equivalent *je m'appelle,* in which at the same time the subject is or stands for the object of the same verb. Rather than calling myself this or that, so am I called by others. To any relationship of the self, even to itself, there is a third party. As the saying goes, it takes two to be one, but three is a crowd: it only adds one loneliness to another.

Even togetherness is not a matter only for lonely individuals. It cannot happen unless—to borrow a comparison of Kierkegaard's—while swimming over seventy thousand fathoms of water one suddenly became conscious, not of one's loneliness, but of the singularity of one's condition as a human being in quest of being human, whether alone or not. Because the singular calls for the universal, singularity does not fold into but defeats dereliction: there is no twig to grab hold of, no writing to grasp, for any kind of help or underwriting—other than one's own self lying in that "no-man's-land" that stretches between "je" and "me," between subject and object, encompassed by one and the same verb, by the word. But then who—the singular excepted—would ever be caught swimming over such an unthinkable body of water?

Ridiculed by his contemporaries, Kierkegaard kept on crying in the wilderness and never quit pointing his finger at "late Christendom," at a church that had lost its soul: the church had lost its soul not for having won but for having lost the world. Preempted from structuring the world to whose worldhood religion must adapt, religion turns into sheer convention; and, its demand frozen into a list of mere dos and don'ts, it voids the least sense of ultimacy of which any human being who, breaking into words, breaks into being human is capable. For we break into being even as we break into faith by breaking into words—by breaking in worlds of this and worlds of that, in the world so loved by God that God gives his only Son. No sooner do we come into the world than we are spoken for. We are spoken for and yet at the same time are set free: we have no choice other than, time and again, to choose. We must swim or sink.

Spoken for, we are embodied. We body forth into words—into faith. History is turned into destiny, language into a world, the word into flesh. And world or flesh is no sooner assumed than our future has no past. Time is what happens now, once and for all. So does destiny or what is left when the past is forgotten or fades into a future it has not expected. Destiny happens once and for all, and not so much because of, as in spite of, the past. It happens now, as does creation, insofar as nothing comes before or after; or as, from alpha to omega, from creation to pleroma, does time that comes and is fulfilled. Worlding the word become flesh, the kingdom of God is at hand (Mark 1:15).

No more than nature holds the key to the creation does history, for Kierkegaard, foster the incarnation or stage Good Friday and Easter. That is exactly what is meant by the tradition, which has the life of Jesus begin with a virgin birth and end with his resurrection or ascension. It is the future of a life without a past, of Jesus as the Christ, the Risen One through whom even the Jew is without a past, unless this past is as empty as the tomb—from which one can only be raised. This is a fiction for which nature cannot account. Nor can history, although it borders on fiction until it does and, paradoxically, must recoil from it for want of establishing the resurrection as a historical fact. Or else the resurrection would hang on the mercy of history. But it does not so hang, any more than it hangs on the mercy of nature. It hangs on the mercy of God and—God being word—is itself the paramount event of language, of the worlding of the word, cosmic as well as existential.

No wonder Kierkegaard is sensitive to Hegel's "system": it too harbors a passion—for the real. It is a passion that, like all passion, is a passion either for God or for the world, and it folds God and the world into one another yet without confusing either of them with the other. It is a passion that, somehow, is common to both Kierkegaard and Hegel—perhaps in spite of them, because neither one would ultimately deny that this passion is also common to both God and the world (as these terms are heard throughout the biblical tradition). It is a passion for the word as well as for the world, whether by way of the rational or by way of faith. No problem. At stake is nothing other than the worlding of the word.

Kierkegaard was not heard, of course. Nor was Hegel. By and large, the establishment showed no sympathy for the knight of faith, if they understood him at all. Likewise, it is a moot question whether those, including noted clergymen, who followed the herald of the rational on the theological slope of his thinking did at all understand him any better. Hegel's admirers simply, and ominously, failed to come to grips with a key item of his agenda—namely, the debunking of an established religion that lagged behind its cultural commitment and confined itself within the protective walls of sacralized structures. They did not realize that his critique of established religion was aimed at the recovery of nothing other than the secular dimension of faith. They went on feeling at ease within the conceptual as well as the institutional model of a sacralized religion, of which Hegel was not less critical than Kierkegaard. It is no wonder that they would also keep missing the point so painstakingly made by the Dane in favor of the religious stage of existence. It is a stage so crucially vulnerable as to call for a commitment, all the more singular for being ultimately contingent upon the secular.

Whether friends of Hegel or foes of Kierkegaard, they were mistaken on two symmetrical counts that coalesced around a religious concern as old as the biblical tradition. It is even as old as religion itself, provided that, out of misbegotten habit, we no longer square religion with the sacred but view it as a groping for that other utopic, and equally if not more fundamental, dimension, whether of life or of faith—in a word, the real. Kierkegaard's spiritual concern with the worldhood of the world is no less concrete than Hegel's concrete concern is less spiritual than Kierkegaard's. They may well have seemed to stand at opposite ends, and somehow Kierkegaard thought he must be at odds with Hegel, and was perhaps mistaken. Obfuscated by the hostility he kept provoking, he presumed that Hegel, for being acclaimed all around, was being better understood. He should have known otherwise. Does not Kierkegaard himself consider the aesthetic and the religious as having one thing in common—namely, the instant, which unlike the good old days can never be sacralized?

In the name of the rational and the secular, or in the name of faith and the religious, and regardless of seemingly antagonistic perspectives, what Hegel and Kierkegaard are denouncing is the specter of a Christian tradition fossilized by institutions that, because they have expelled the spiritual no less than the rational, have lost touch with the real. They are not credible, either from the standpoint of reason or from that of faith. But, curiously, for both Kierkegaard and Hegel, the real is not enough; it is not quite all that is the case because it never is quite real enough through itself alone. That is, it cannot feed on thought alone any more than it can feed on belief alone. It lies at their intersection, where being human is what a human being is all about, where one has yet to account and speak up for the way one is spoken for.

Faith is a passion. A gripping echo of this assertion of Kierkegaard's can still be heard through Jaspers's down-to-earth definition of faith as a mode of being. Both Kierkegaard and Jaspers seem to shun the mystical, but they have a common concern. And this concern is one that, braced as it may be, whether by faith or by reason, is geared to an ethic. It is an ethic as ineluctable as it is improbable because the passion it is folded by is no more impassioned with itself than the being of which it is a mode consists in climbing up or down some ladder of being. Because no moral act can be authenticated by mere activism, this ethic does not rely on any kind of prop made up of escalating values. Nor does it appeal to any principle above and beyond itself by which it would be authenticated. Making room for no exception, it would be a straitjacket. Self-authenticating, it could result only in a self-justifying code of dos and don'ts—the very denial of an ethic of faith. An ethic of faith is not so much borne out by deeds (though they may well speak louder than words) as it consists in bearing out words of which deeds are born.

A Gratuitous Ethic

An ethic of faith is an ethic of language. It is a gratuitous ethic. It is so gratuitous that, articulated in the language of faith, it bears out a basic experience of life: no one *deserves* being justified, just as no human being can draw any merit from being human, from doing what ought or ought not to be done. It is not a self-authenticating but a self-exposing ethic. It consists in resisting the ultimate temptation—that of being grounded, or of milling a prescription. It does not spell out a code but tells a parable—and the parable itself tells no moral of a story but enacts a scenario,[1] which lays the ground for a new act. It plots a new world. As Amos N. Wilder keenly points out, "[T]he world plot plays itself over [. . .], yet in such a way that it is always *unprecedented*."[2] Rather than merely telling the allegory of a world that is all that is the case, the parable points to what, falling into place, is itself limited to no place. Rather than remembering, it anticipates: it remembers only what it can hope for. It hangs on a tropological, even proleptic, deconstruction of that which is only to be realized, and accomplished, and fulfilled so long as it is and never can be real all by itself and on its own grounds.[3] A parable does not tell a past event. It does not repeat the past. It repeats what has not taken place, what has not yet happened. Nothing comes before the worlding of the word.

Lacan's sentence, indeed, bears out this biblical insight: the order of the world is a word order. Even should perchance the world be all that is the case, as Wittgenstein avers, no fact is a fact except through the ministrations of a language, of words ordained, though not self-ordained, to that effect. No world comes about that is not wrapped up in words—words through which facts are handled and yet, without being manhandled, are tipped into fiction.[4] These are words that alone are capable of a metaphor. No world comes about that is not wrapped up in a parable, a worlding of words whose meaning is all the more symbolic for being literally true. In the Lord's Supper, bread is all the more symbolic for being real bread instead of a reconstituted chemical, industrial, commercial, and, to top it all, tasteless substitute for it.

Tillich notwithstanding, the question is not whether the literal is more or less than the symbolic[5] but whether there can be anything too literal for becoming symbolic. The question is whether the literal, which is neither more nor less than the symbolic, is literal enough to be symbolic. As with Einstein's equation when it pervades the public imagination, truth is a function of the metaphoricity of the literal. This metaphoricity is not added to the literal but is given with it. This is the same metaphoricity that also precludes the symbolic from upstaging the literal. Nothing is more symbolic than the literal, and nothing is more literal than that which calls for a symbol. The literal is not merely literal. Like an empty tomb, it is what is left of the power of a symbol that has been shed of its power of congruence with the real. It is what becomes of the incarnation when it is resolved into the midpoint of time instead of pointing to its linguistic milieu. The times are fulfilled and the word is worlded when the literal is so literal as to become symbolic, and the world of facts becomes a fiction of the worlding of the word, a parable of the kingdom.

Of themselves facts cannot raise a thought. In Ricoeur's celebrated phrase, only a symbol can give rise to it, only a symbol can beget it by parting the literal and the spiritual, or the religious and the cultural, from one another even while assuming that each has a part in the other, that is, by letting words part with themselves to the extent that language is not so much rooted in as it is seeded from words. Only words can break out into language through which symbols are broken in—and split, if only because language is itself split between I and Thou even as between subject and object: no symbol is broken in through language that is not ultimately a broken symbol.

Symbols are broken: they are not empowered by nature or by history but only by language, through which even rules are symbolic above all.

Rules make room for action, for interaction—for that which, because they claim to be normative, is unprecedented. And they are normative, that is, groundbreaking, even as rules must be, if the covenant their ethic is supposed to attest is not to be reduced to mere convention. Grounded on this or that convention only, rules will end up being "grounded" and denounced for their collusion with this or that convention.

In contrast to past-oriented conventions, a covenant looks forward to the future. Geared to the inauguration of a new deal, no covenant is permanent that is not also permanently put into question. It is constituted by that of which it is itself constitutive: an exception to the rule. To wit: the very notion of Israel as a chosen people. Neither nature nor history had predisposed Israel to that privilege—none at least that Israel deserved. And nothing that came before could justify it. Nothing comes before a covenant even as nothing comes before creation. Likewise, it is not nature or history but language that delimits the timing of the covenant and its ethical space. It delimits the ethic through which the covenant is put to the test and attested. Language is the realm of ethic as it is that of faith.

As Socrates used to say, "The unexamined life is not worth living." Nothing different is meant by the biblical tradition when it repeats, "The righteous shall live by faith."[6] Once and for all. In spite of one's antecedents. Regardless of the outcome (as implied by the parable of the Last Judgment). The righteous self is therefore an autonomous self: should it lie in God, it does not rely on God as on a pair of crutches; it needs no safety net. Or else it would have traded its autonomy for the heteronomy of a self-righteous self. Unlike the heteronomous self, the autonomous self is a vulnerable self—so vulnerable as to be singular and to shun being exemplary (i.e., ethically correct).

An ethic of faith is no faith in ethics. An ethics that aims at the universal is an ethic that bypasses the singular. A mere system, it forgets what the legend of Rabbi Zusiah keeps reminding us—namely, that in the life of faith, the universal coincides with the singular.[7] Faith does not fan uniformity. We have in common what makes each of us unique. We are unique to the extent of what we have in common—a language, which never belies the self that lies in it. Even as language is never so local as to be parochial and shy away from the universal, so also the self is never so individual as to be incommunicado, confined within itself. No one speaks who is not spoken for. Solidarity is at stake in the singular, and because the converse is also true, solidarity is what can alone prevent the universal from sinking into uniformity, a mere veil meant to conceal newfangled hierarchies and no less equally subdued heteronomies.

I must here take a risk and seem to drive a wedge between faith as a passion and faith as a mode of being. I also incur yet another risk by suggesting, through an oversimplification, that the biblical tradition is more prone to identifying God with language, with faith as language, than with the language of being. Like the self, even God is understood not in terms of "being" but in terms of "wording." Put differently, in the biblical tradition, a being is what goes by a name.[8] It has been sold out, so to speak. Beings are therefore heteronomous: once Adam named all the cattle and the birds of the air and every beast of the field, there was yet no one who could be called woman. In that legend, as in the prologue of John, the word does not become a being, it becomes flesh. In contrast to the heteronomous order of being, the order of "wording" is autonomous. It has no name for God except by antiphrasis. God is no being but a word. God is no being but wording—and lies in that power of wording of which language is the instrument. God is language, and it is only in the hands of language that God, being no God per se, becomes God for Abraham, and again for Isaac, and again for Jacob—a nameless God, as Jesus attests when, to the dismay of his hearers, he declares, "Before Abraham was, I am." For these hearers, this ultimate expression of Jesus's faith can only conceal a faith that does not lead to God—to their kind of God. It is a name, not a language, not the word.

For them, faith has indeed no alternative but to lead to God. But this God, being no more than a being, be it the highest, is a God whose power overshadows and would colonize the power of language. Hence an inevitable question: it arises as to which, God or faith, takes the other hostage. Is faith that can only lead to God still faith? Or does it, rather, point then to a principle of segregation, at least between believers and unbelievers, in the light of which rules, instead of being confirmed by the exception, serve to exempt from their application?

Enforced by language alone, faith borders on unfaith, just as the religious borders on the secular, and conversely. Faith happens as do words of a language whose verb they no more command than they are commanded by. Unlike the flu, no sooner is one caught by faith than one is caught dead and brought to life, and one is spoken for. Rather than a mystique of the supernatural, faith entails and blossoms in an ethic, the morality of which pretends to nothing more than being dis-appointed and put into question by the very practice to which it resorts. We inherit an ethic. We do not inherit faith. Ethics, because it appeals to the transmissibility of its object, is like ancestry bound to become irrelevant or repetitious; it partakes of the ritual, beyond the purview of which it confronts us with a task we can only leap into—by faith. Although faith itself, "if it has no works, is dead" (or is "a lifeless thing," if "it does not lead to action"),[9] it is not, however, exhausted and much less justified by them. Nor is its ethical relevance deflected by any language whose performance, once sacralized, would as it were take it into custody. Rituals are in the custody of a language. Faith is not. We do not inherit faith. We live by it, and it is nothing that we can bequeath—as Jesus reminds us when, keeping to the sabbatical ethic of the Old Testament and daring to turn language upside down, he declares, "Before Abraham was, I am." In the same breath, he both desacralizes ethics and secularizes faith.[10]

Jesus does not quite invent the secular. It was already adumbrated by Israel's notion of creation as well as by its conception of the law, not to mention the so-called code of holiness. In contrast with other religions and their spiritualistic shunning of things material, the charge of materialism is leveled at Israel's approach to life and the basic experience of it. It will not spare Christianity, either. In contrast to the ethic of other religions, Israel's is basically a world-affirming, not a world-denying, ethic. It honors the secular.

At the very least, it did so long before modernity came around. But we have since been led to believe that the secularization of faith resulted from the intellectual upheaval culminating in the irresistible primacy of reason. We forget that, on both a religious and a cultural level, the Christian tradition had already—with Saint Thomas, among others—seeded the future autonomy of the secular as well as of reason, each being a necessary dimension of the design for a moral order of the world. It fostered by the same token an increasing awareness of its own secularity. Succinctly put, it was even tipped from worldly concerns lobbying for heavenly realities to heavenly concerns lobbying for earthly realities, from the religious into the cultural and its willy-nilly synonym, the secular. More scientifically put, it will be tipped from a mythological to a scientific technological universe of discourse, however characterized by either ideological or utopian considerations.

Admittedly, aside from Thomas More and Thomas Müntzer, beyond New Harmony and the Amish, the Christian tradition has shown some reluctance in switching from the sacred to utopia as the framework of its ethic of faith. But it has at least not refrained from letting go of a purely naturalistic approach to religion and, though somewhat subconsciously, has intimated a switch to language as the proper medium for understanding both the world and the self, or God.[11] No longer does religion appear in need of fanning some would-be objective order like that of nature or its variant, history.[12] More significantly, it is swayed even less by either the necessitarianism so typical of the former or the fatalism of the latter. Odd as this may sound, driven through a tunnel, religion had to come out. When it does, it has come of age. Moving beyond the occlusion of time and eternity, it discovers historicity just as the Middle Ages had come up with the temporal or its twin, the secular. However inchoately, religion already thrives on that which can happen at all if it happens also to me. Religion thrives on the ephemeral—on that which happens once and for all. Call it time, or eternity. It does not matter.

Obviously, like that of any human being, the life of Jesus also proceeds between a birth and a death. But from the cradle to the empty tomb, it spreads out and unfolds as the starkest denial of any quest for roots in some anamnestic experience of life, funded by (albeit religiously) sacralized prerogatives pegged whether on nature or on history. To the carpenter's son from Nazareth, all of that is no more than a fiction, though not to be discarded. It is a fiction of which, nevertheless, he is the central figure. And nothing raises a question about our ultimate concern better than a fiction.

Unlike a scientific theory, a fiction never replaces another fiction. A scientific theory survives its usefulness only to the extent that it becomes a fiction: we still refer to the sun as rising. Fictions work so long as they are relevant, and they are relevant to the extent that they work. For us, the sun goes on rising and setting, although Ptolemy's universe—his metafiction—has been replaced, say, by Einstein's. Or to paraphrase W. H. Auden, seas in their vastness are nameless; only ports have names for them. Similarly, through Jesus we have a name for the nameless God, and yet God remains nameless. Through the life of Jesus we have a parable of God's holiness, of God's otherness. Emblematically, the life of Jesus embodies a faith so radical and so radically free of all claims as to loom all the more glorious for exposing (rather than imposing) itself through what, humanly speaking, amounts to an inimitable and equally improbable ethic—and, moreover, to an ethic of the secular. Or, in Bonhoeffer's celebrated formula, it amounts to an ethic of a world come of age. It is an ethic for the worldhood of that world so loved by God as to be God's utopia[13] and, beyond all religious apartheid, to concern both Israel and the nations.

The tree that falls in the middle of the forest needs no one to witness the sound it makes. Saying it does make a sound is a fiction. In a court of justice the authority of a witness is a fiction: the witness is there only to show that, though he was present on the scene, he need not have been present for the event to have taken place. So also is the ethic of faith a fiction that needs no one to witness the difference it makes. Symbolic, the difference is all the more real. The ethic of faith would in no way be religious were its impact not secular—as unconscious of itself as God, rather than being this or that god, is an anonymous god.

The Death of God and the Ambiguities of the Secular

> ... secularized (should this word have any meaning elsewhere than in the religious tradition it maintains while pretending to be freed from it).
>
> —Jacques Derrida, *Foi et savoir, suivi de Le siècle et le pardon*

Symbols die. Metaphors become clichés. The road to language is paved with dead tongues—those witnesses to the secular downloading of languages that once enchanted the world. The same applies to the worlding of the word characteristic of biblical religion. Once downloaded, its ultimate metaphor, God, looks superannuated, an old-fashioned garment, a filling, a stopgap, and as useless as buttons on coat sleeves. And yet nothing is less allergic to religion than language, however dissonant or secularized. Were it not for the secular and its ambiguities, not only the imperial Christianity it survives but also God (who is and is not) would be defunct.

In an essay on possible theological inklings of the human predicament in our so-called postmodern situation, Robert P. Scharlemann is intent on delineating a method that would prevent them from unnecessarily clashing with or lagging too far behind postmodern assumptions. Rather receptive to the rhetoric of deconstruction proposals, he maps out their impact upon the theological agenda. Scharlemann points to the markers through whose conspiracy-like constellation theology is put in jeopardy, unless it is willing to bring itself radically into question.[1]

The Religious Meaning of the Secular: Language and the Self

Less concerned with the first half of this subhead, Scharlemann naturally begins with the self. However it is defined, he points out that there is no self independently of the linguistic milieu by which it is molded. Besides, languages differ from one another so radically that at times their respective lexicons seem impermeable to one another. They defeat any attempt at a harmonious one-to-one correspondence between one language and another. Yet they also corroborate the fact that, regardless of the milieu in which our basic experience of life takes place, it is a unique experience. This is not because experience folds back upon itself, but because it is bound up with a linguistic milieu that may be impermeable to another and, hence, cannot host it. Linguistic milieus can be simply inhospitable if not outright allergic to one another. We are unique, but only by virtue of blinders, of not being able to see beyond our nose. In other words, I am conscious of this uniqueness only because I have no access to my unconscious.

In a more polished language, Scharlemann underlines the two characters of this first marker. On the one hand, he writes that "the self is not transparent to itself because consciousness has no direct access to the realm of the unconscious"; and, on the other, somewhat surprisingly, he draws from this that "there is an irreducible duality in the structure of subjectivity which makes the self pluralistic rather than universal in character." But does Scharlemann not overlook two things?

One of them is that, at least with Lacan, unfathomable as the unconscious may be, it is no less construed as a language. We may seem not to have access to it. Does it follow that it has no access to our consciousness? We speak, and to that same extent we are spoken for. Conscious or unconscious, language is our host. And so far as it is hospitable, linguistic hospitality is a pipe dream if it stops at the door of another linguistic milieu. Scharlemann is more sensitive to Babel than to Pentecost. But the clash of languages he seems to magnify makes short shrift of the notion that no language is foreign to another, just as no religion is foreign to another so long as what they are ideologically separated by does not overshadow and extenuate what they have in common—namely, the secular.

The other thing overlooked has to do with Scharlemann's contention that, because the self is split from itself, subjectivity can at best be pluralistic rather than universal. But what is the reason for restraining subjectivity to pluralism? And how is the difference from the universal to be construed?

Is it a matter of degree? Moreover, how does it square with Scharlemann's understanding of subjectivity, which, he says, is an instance of every subject and yet is itself subject to the "duality" by which subjectivity is constituted? And if it does square with it, why should the pluralistic option be the only one, especially if by duality is obviously meant no dualism of any kind but rather something akin to "alterity"—possibly even something like the binary language of computers? On this point, Scharlemann should make up his mind and adjudicate the issue at stake either in terms of the conflict of the One and the Many or in terms of the singular and the universal as poles of mutual hospitality.

Mutually playing host to one another, the singular and the universal need not collapse into one another. They do not need to eclipse one another, either. They may even overlap and, paradoxically, it is to the extent to which they do overlap that they are both contingent on one another and yet autonomous vis-à-vis one another. Because of their mutual contingency, the singular and the universal are preserved from the opacity that would otherwise threaten their respective autonomy by "freezing," as it were, the specificity of their respective linguistic milieus. A matter of language and therefore of consciousness, this opacity is not different from the opacity of the self to itself and, a fortiori, of language to another language if not to itself. And yet only the singular can lay claim to the universal (rather than to mere pluralism), just as no language is universal unless nothing is universal that is not construed as a language. Every language has the potential of a metalanguage. Or else we should not have the least consciousness of the uniqueness of our basic experience of life; and the linguistic milieu to which we owe the characteristics of our subjectivity should turn into a linguistic dead end. As for the self, cheated out of its life milieu between subject and object, it should be reduced to a single monad.

From Kant to Heidegger, metaphysics peters out.[2] Ontotheism scuttles itself. The debacle does not unmoor Scharlemann. Not even a detour by way of Hegel and Nietzsche helps him to obviate his analysis of a self split from itself and more or less sentenced to lick its wound. A widening gap continues to yawn between the natural and the supernatural, the noumenal and the phenomenal. The atomization of the subject waxes under the growing consciousness of an "I" barred from ever reducing any "Thou" to another "I."[3] We belong to linguistic milieus whose respective perspectival differences do not mesh and render such a task impossible. This amounts to claiming, reversing Buber's insight, that unless God can be expressed, there is no point in addressing him; or that the subjective I-Thou relation annuls the objective I-It relations (which Buber never claims); or, again, that the former lies within language and the latter without. In fact, all this amounts to is a subtle and self-defeating suggestion that we can go on operating with the traditional tools of our linguistic milieus, even though these tools have been blunted in one of two ways or both: either because the order of the world is a word order but there is no word that becomes flesh and encompasses the subjective and the objective, the religious and the secular; or because there can be no world whose worldhood can host the worlding of the word. At this point, it is as if the dynamics of the incarnation had been defeated by its own rhetoric.

Instead of God emptying himself, it is now language that is emptied of itself. It does not survive the death of God. Nor does it survive, in Charles E. Winquist's phrase, "the silence of the real,"[4] its adiaphoricity, any more than it does the silence of God, as Jacques Ellul would put it. Not only no flesh is available that would or could even host such a God, but also nothing is literal enough to be raised up into the realm of a symbolic language through the metonymic interplay of words habilitated to fill the gap between thought and being or between spirit and nature. And, by the same token, between the religious and the secular—between the vertical dimension of the incarnation and its horizontal dimension. The soteriological overtones of the incarnation muffle the eschatological design of its innermost intention. The worlding of the word as horizontal dimension of the incarnation is defrauded by its vertical dimension, the saving word; the eschatological is shortchanged by the soteriological.

But this subtle substitution of a self-emptying language for the classic self-emptying of God serves only to muddle the issue. It shifts the focus from the eschatological dynamics of the incarnation as dialectic of the religious and the secular back to the sacred as determinant of the linguistic milieu of faith. By foreclosing the secular, it so cleaves the worlding of the word from the saving word that "Only a God can save us," as a speechless Heidegger sums it all up with this famous sentence borrowed from Hölderlin—except that, according to the biblical tradition, the God that saves us is a God that makes room for us even as the God that creates is a God that makes room for the world. Pedestrian as this way of putting it may be and insolence notwithstanding, one cannot in this respect help but recall Hegel's situation vis-à-vis the theological authorities of his time. They were for the most part engaged in a type of neoscholastic speculation about the faith of the church. They were concerned, not so much with its relevance to the social and spiritual conditions of their day, as with its affiliation with a tradition whose linguistic milieu was lagging behind the evolution of the modern world. Still, Hegel somehow shares with them the potent symbolics of Good Friday. It is the day on which, even for Luther, existential poet turned theologian, God himself dies, nailed to a cross.

Something of this tragic sense of life pervades Hegel's appropriation of the theme. But it does not serve only for the uplifting of souls on the verge of tears. Its religious dimension subsides, undiminished, but it is developed into a challenge to the secular world. It is secularized. It is turned into a world historical process. All the same, it also belies the historical process, through which it has, as it were, been split from itself. As Scharlemann points out, the incarnation appears "as the point at which Spirit is most estranged from itself." But then as ultimate emblem of the self-emptying, whether of God or of the spirit and of language, the tomb itself is empty, and the flesh has nonetheless been restored to its spiritual design, religion to its secular obligation, and the world to its worldhood—to the secular.

Healing is not only psychic, it is also somatic; the concretion of salvation lies in the concretion of the redeeming word. Whether salvation is from Bethlehem or from Nazareth,[5] whether it means being saved *from* God or *from* man, or for that matter by God if not in spite of God, Jesus is not obsessed with salvation;[6] he is concerned with the kingdom of God, with the worlding of the word, and therefore with the religious as well as the secular dimension of its linguistic milieu.

With modernity, however, it is not so much the spirit as language that is estranged from itself. It must choose between faith and reason, between the literal and the spiritual, and, in spite of Schleiermacher's protests against the cultural despisers of religion, it becomes infatuated either with the religious or with the secular. At home with neither, language is dragged and pulled apart by their respective deviations, fundamentalism on the one hand and secularism on the other. Whether under the aegis of a throbbing reason or in the throes of Kierkegaard's "late Christendom," it is so haunted by the spectacle of what is mistaken for a disenchanted world that it readily embraces the equally lenifying comfort either of fideism or of secularism, at least until it spawns so-called postmodern rhetoric.

Unlike modernity, postmodern thought is not haunted by secularism. Nor is it haunted by any kind of rigid atheism that would have survived the death of God. Fiddling with the cathartic and, at bottom, no less self-religious divisions are tolerated only so far as they are conspicuously internalized and unconditionally confined within the private realm. These divisions have become obsolete—at least so far as pluralism is a fait accompli and its underlying secular assumption is kept from adumbrating the horizon of theological discourse. Appeals to the profane are all the more convenient for being alluring.

But by downgrading the secular and identifying it with the profane, or alternately by first logging the secular in together with the artificial and subordinating it to technology, does Tillich not in fact turn the secular into his own unacknowledged bête noire? Despite the diversity of its facets, this is a question that, raised against the background of his method of the correlation between religion and culture, harks back to his own notion of the *kairos* as a prophetic occasion for both faith and the world, each reconciled with itself, to be reconciled with one another. Tillich is even more explicit. In keeping with the prophetic spirit, he states that not only faith and the world but also both "the sacramental and the critical attitudes are united in the consciousness of the kairos."[10] Still not in sight is any mention at all of the religious and the secular, a pair from which Tillich recoils. This pair could just as well stand for sacramental and critical and should logically pop up at this juncture, but it does not.[11]

Instead, Tillich's theology of culture falls back on the primacy of nature, even as, in his systematic theology, the symbolism of faith is eclipsed by the soteriological supranaturalism of ontology. Failing to elaborate the prophetic consciousness of the *kairos* as the dialectic link of the religious and the secular, he isolates the former and diminishes the latter; he does not see that a theology of culture like his own demands a theology of the word, not a theology of being. The God that is and is being itself eclipses the biblical God that speaks. This God and the idol have too much in common to subvert one another or even to bear comparison with one another. Silence alone would result from it, whether of God or of the real. Or else, in the Old Testament, why does God always complain, asking, "With whom will you compare me?"[12] Could the reason simply be that God no more than the idol, or that death no less than life, "are held in hand by language?"[13] If so, could that be because through language, even sidereal silence, whether of God or of the real, not to mention the world itself, is both desacralized and dedivinized,[14] and as shown by the parables of Jesus, "religion becomes secular without loss"?[15]

The Secular and Ellul's Overestimation of the Sacred

Here, possibly, lies also the reason why, with Jacques Ellul, an aura of suspicion equally shrouds both pluralism and the secular. No matter how secularized today's society may be, Ellul contends that it exhibits "the same religious organization as one finds in traditional societies, together with a system of relationship that, involving the sacred, the myths, the religions, coordinates them all into a sacral world."[16] Resting on a naturalistic approach, a sacral world rests on the assumption that nature acts upon us rather than being acted upon.[17]

Although today what acts upon us rather than being acted upon is not so much nature as it is technology, our world is no less sacral: it has merely swapped one myth for another and nature for technology. Whether or not, in this process, nature is restored and returned to its integrity is another matter. The point is that we remain fascinated with the sacred—to such an extent that today "the desacralization of nature, of the cosmos and of the remaining traditional religious objects immediately gives way to the sacralization of society by technology,"[18] even though technology has been a major factor in desacralizing our natural milieu. As a result, ours is a society that, on the one hand, seeks to adorn itself with the mantle of the sacred and, on the other, is becoming more and more technicized—and less and less reassuring. For all its pervasiveness, our technological milieu is no more comprehensible, no more significant, than the natural milieu ever was. We yearn for some meaning, for the origin of it all, "that is, for the sacred."[19]

All of this holds together, no doubt. But we should not underestimate the latent hint of a paradox in the conclusion Ellul draws by contending that this world of ours is not as secular as we pretend it to be—or even, perhaps, as we would wish it to be. On the one hand, in spite of the widely broadcast idea that technology has been a desacralizing factor, our technological society is even more addicted to the sacred. On the other hand, while acknowledging that "the sacred is not identical with the religious," Ellul readily concedes that, by and large, "the sacred overflows religious phenomena, and that religion is thus one of the possible translations of the sacred."[20]

Regardless of their attachment or indifference to a metaphysics of presence, Tillich and Ellul, like Heidegger, live in a disenchanted world, as Max Weber's famous and no less intrinsically misleading phrase would have it. They do not live in a secular world—in the *saecula saeculorum*. The emptying power of language, it is haunted by the loss of its religious dimension. It is haunted by the sacred—not by the holy, with which the sacred is often confused.[7] Even in biblical times, getting rid of the sacred was more easily said than done, in spite of the Decalogue and the thoroughgoing secular dimension of the commitment expected of the chosen people by the God of Israel, expected of a nation hardly identified as owner of a piece of land and even less as the people of a book.

Lurking behind every landmark of history and of our collective memory, the sacred even seizes and bends our very capacity for speech and distorts every step of our enfranchisement from history as well as from nature; it pervades and, ravishing language itself, recasts it in its own image, turning it into a most appropriately so-called landmark of the hegemony it claims over all that is. To wit: so many tropes from Mother Earth to the Book of Nature by way of gods that die and rise again. Turning language into the instrument of a quest, be it that of the Holy Grail or that of the historical Jesus, the sacred hands the quest over to a task of mere inventory rather than of invention and keeps it from doing a new thing, keeps it from worlding the word. Of course, this caricature is not meant to exhaust the postmodern rhetoric. Far from it. What is denounced is the rhetoric, not the content. For all our love affair with the postmodern rhetoric, some of us manage to remain considerably old-fashioned. "Only a god can save us." But allusions to such a god are more often than not overshadowed by overtones of its sociological surrogate, the sacred.[8]

Against this background, the time has come to proceed by weaving together reflections culled from reading three authors not usually cited in the same breath: Paul Tillich, Jacques Ellul, and Richard Rorty. At first blush, the only thing they seem to have in common is that all three survey the same landscape as it gradually shifts from one hue to another under the postmodern spotlight.

Diverse they certainly are. But what they have in common shows in their attitude toward the "secular." Even if Tillich is in the main sensitive to it, Ellul is, by contrast, largely suspicious of it, while Rorty is not only rather reconciled with it but also even somewhat of a zealous advocate of it.

The overall presuppositions of Tillich's systematic theology give his discourse a different tenor from the postmodern as the latter is customarily understood. But no one can deny that his theology of culture, apart from evincing affinity for this so-called postmodern posture, even adumbrates it, albeit perhaps somewhat elliptically.

At the other extreme, commanding the whole field of Rorty's impenitent vision, the secular has even a flavor of its own. Seemingly evincing no hangover from past reliance on a religious appraisal of the world, Rorty's understanding of the secular is so secular that, paradoxically, upon further elaboration, it boldly operates in like manner as that which, with Tillich, culminates in the Protestant principle. But it does so with this major difference: Rorty adamantly keeps from indulging any kind of impulsive intrusion in the name of some heavenly authority. He does this for a simple yet highly discriminating reason: the human venture is, because of its contingency, much too humbling a cause for anyone to try to fall back on anything less contingent.

Between Tillich and Rorty and by comparison with them, Ellul admittedly cuts a strange figure. Thoroughly cognizant of the foibles as well as other idiosyncratic delusions afloat in today's world, he sticks to a language that, on the one hand, has all the appearances of being untutored. On the other hand, this language is, at least "officially," so uncontaminated by any jargon, linked or not to postmodern discourse, that it nevertheless allows him to develop an approach to the ethic of faith, which for being "biblical" is, according to Ellul, all the more sensitive to the human predicament. It calls, not for a new sacralization of our social reconstructions and their cortege of collective or individual self-serving interests, but for the "sanctification" (hallowing) of both God and this world of God's making.

One last remark before moving on to a more detailed testing of their respective contributions. What separates Ellul from Rorty is, oddly enough, the secular: while it blends with language for the latter, it is for the former sunk in the indifference of a world orphaned by the silence of God. What separates both of them from Tillich is, no less oddly, the religious insofar as it resonates with the natural—a surcharge, superfluous for Rorty, illicit for Ellul.

Religion Denatured: Tillich's Underestimation of the Secular

Possibly even more attractive than Tillich's thoroughgoing systematic exhibition of the Christian faith is the groundbreaking analysis through which he redefines the relation between a culture and its religion as well as between a religion and its culture and shows how this reciprocity culminates in a symmetrical display of so-called Protestant principle and Catholic substance. Bound to clash with one another, substance and principle as well as religion and culture seem equally bound to mutual healing.

Struck by the depth and the amplitude of his thought, one is naturally deterred from seeking a soft spot out of which to pick some possibly faltering signs in the cogency of an otherwise apparently well-sealed argument. In desperation, one is even tempted to look for them in the margins of his thought—in the fact, for example, that in contrast to the traditional love affair between Protestantism and music (if not painting), Tillich clearly opts for architecture. It elevates us above and beyond mere nature. It can also remind us of our being contingent upon it. It has an ontological quality, ever more rarely reverberated even by, or especially by, other avant-garde expressions of modern art. Perhaps it differs from them because, in its impact on the secular dimension of life in a technological world, it never ceases to remind us of nature as our normal habitat without reminding us that, for Tillich, symbols, however sophisticated, are rooted in nature.

But a shift has occurred. Bemoaning it, Tillich never refrains from pointing out that, with the increasing impact of the Judeo-Christian tradition, religion, deflecting from its former naturalistic approach, surrenders to a process that finally denatures it. Detached from the rich symbolism fostered by nature, we have become addicted to a technological, and artificial, proliferation of signs. In the past, religion dealt with building up nature into a concern about the ultimate; now, in contrast with this ultimate preoccupation, it convoys mere preoccupations, rather mundane and all too secular.

Possibly legitimate in their own rank, such secular preoccupations distract us from the task usually ascribed to a religion geared to an ultimate concern. The self is not only prevented from being gathered, and unified, and centered; but also, consequently, even as we move from Tillich's earliest to his latest writings, it is disrupted the more it becomes entangled in the discountenancing grip of a pluralistic universe of thought and belief. In the earlier phase, the Christian faith is at stake in confronting socialism and the question of social justice. In the later phase, it must cope with subtler and all the more disorienting effects of its encounter with other world religions.

From Germany to America, from an expanding universe of discourse to the shrinking world of electronic communication, Tillich's own perspective reflects this shift by shifting in turn from "secular" to "pluralism" as the key word for assessing this evolving human predicament. Discreet as this shift may be, it raises suspicion about the way in which this factual reference to pluralism is conveniently inserted in Tillich's overall argument. It overshadows the eminently theological question of the secular and even sweeps it under the purview of what for him amounts to a paganizing secularism—a distortion if not an outright denial of the world-affirming (i.e., secular) dimension of the ethic of faith.

Pluralism itself, as the early Christians had already discovered, is not necessarily world affirming. And they rightly contended that, in the Roman Empire, it was not what they really had or wanted to have in common with adherents of other religions. What they had in common is what this very pluralism occulted—the secular, a prefiguration of the world come of age, if not of the world to come. Now, once again, in this technological situation of ours, a similar pluralism is flourishing. And again, no less obviously, the secular is the only thing we all have in common. As aware of the general contours of the issue as Tillich doubtless was, it is a moot question whether he tackles it or glosses it over.

But when he writes about the future of religion, Tillich points out that, in order for it to mesh and be consonant with a changing world, no encompassing language will emerge unless it develops a religious dimension capable of coping with whatever symbolic inkling it encounters in the realm of the "profane."[9] Underline that term. Deliberately used here, whether in contrast to secular or as its symbolically more turgid synonym, "profane" is in German a word of which Tillich has always been singularly fond. Also fond of it were other thinkers of that period, including Jacques Maritain, who moreover advocates a sort of "buffer zone" that, though placed under the joint authority of the sacred and the profane, radically separates them from one another. Maritain is not concerned with the secular, or with the acculturation of religion. His interest lies with what, subsequently, assigning religion to the role of a mole of sorts, neological Vatican jargon will label "inculturation."

By comparison, Tillich's approach is far from being as hierarchical and as somewhat condescending toward the world. But his approach does not quite alleviate the impression that of the profane one cannot, as one might of the secular, say that it has or ever will come of age. Tillich's approach is even shy of wakening his reader to the notion that, in a pluralistic world, what separates us is religion; or that in the public domain shared by all, religious divisions are tolerated only so far as they are conspicuously internalized and unconditionally confined within the private realm. These divisions have become obsolete—at least so far as pluralism is a fait accompli and its underlying secular assumption is kept from adumbrating the horizon of theological discourse. Appeals to the profane are all the more convenient for being alluring.

But by downgrading the secular and identifying it with the profane, or alternately by first logging the secular in together with the artificial and subordinating it to technology, does Tillich not in fact turn the secular into his own unacknowledged bête noire? Despite the diversity of its facets, this is a question that, raised against the background of his method of the correlation between religion and culture, harks back to his own notion of the *kairos* as a prophetic occasion for both faith and the world, each reconciled with itself, to be reconciled with one another. Tillich is even more explicit. In keeping with the prophetic spirit, he states that not only faith and the world but also both "the sacramental and the critical attitudes are united in the consciousness of the kairos."[10] Still not in sight is any mention at all of the religious and the secular, a pair from which Tillich recoils. This pair could just as well stand for sacramental and critical and should logically pop up at this juncture, but it does not.[11]

Instead, Tillich's theology of culture falls back on the primacy of nature, even as, in his systematic theology, the symbolism of faith is eclipsed by the soteriological supranaturalism of ontology. Failing to elaborate the prophetic consciousness of the *kairos* as the dialectic link of the religious and the secular, he isolates the former and diminishes the latter; he does not see that a theology of culture like his own demands a theology of the word, not a theology of being. The God that is and is being itself eclipses the biblical God that speaks. This God and the idol have too much in common to subvert one another or even to bear comparison with one another. Silence alone would result from it, whether of God or of the real. Or else, in the Old Testament, why does God always complain, asking, "With whom will you compare me?"[12] Could the reason simply be that God no more than the idol, or that death no less than life, "are held in hand by language?"[13] If so, could that be because through language, even sidereal silence, whether of God or of the real, not to mention the world itself, is both desacralized and dedivinized,[14] and as shown by the parables of Jesus, "religion becomes secular without loss"?[15]

The Secular and Ellul's Overestimation of the Sacred

Here, possibly, lies also the reason why, with Jacques Ellul, an aura of suspicion equally shrouds both pluralism and the secular. No matter how secularized today's society may be, Ellul contends that it exhibits "the same religious organization as one finds in traditional societies, together with a system of relationship that, involving the sacred, the myths, the religions, coordinates them all into a sacral world."[16] Resting on a naturalistic approach, a sacral world rests on the assumption that nature acts upon us rather than being acted upon.[17]

Although today what acts upon us rather than being acted upon is not so much nature as it is technology, our world is no less sacral: it has merely swapped one myth for another and nature for technology. Whether or not, in this process, nature is restored and returned to its integrity is another matter. The point is that we remain fascinated with the sacred—to such an extent that today "the desacralization of nature, of the cosmos and of the remaining traditional religious objects immediately gives way to the sacralization of society by technology,"[18] even though technology has been a major factor in desacralizing our natural milieu. As a result, ours is a society that, on the one hand, seeks to adorn itself with the mantle of the sacred and, on the other, is becoming more and more technicized—and less and less reassuring. For all its pervasiveness, our technological milieu is no more comprehensible, no more significant, than the natural milieu ever was. We yearn for some meaning, for the origin of it all, "that is, for the sacred."[19]

All of this holds together, no doubt. But we should not underestimate the latent hint of a paradox in the conclusion Ellul draws by contending that this world of ours is not as secular as we pretend it to be—or even, perhaps, as we would wish it to be. On the one hand, in spite of the widely broadcast idea that technology has been a desacralizing factor, our technological society is even more addicted to the sacred. On the other hand, while acknowledging that "the sacred is not identical with the religious," Ellul readily concedes that, by and large, "the sacred overflows religious phenomena, and that religion is thus one of the possible translations of the sacred."[20]

Regardless of their attachment or indifference to a metaphysics of presence, Tillich and Ellul, like Heidegger, live in a disenchanted world, as Max Weber's famous and no less intrinsically misleading phrase would have it. They do not live in a secular world—in the *saecula saeculorum*. The world that, for Tillich, is threatened by the demonic remains infested by the sacred for Ellul. It either harks back to or is swayed and overpowered by the sacred. Pluralism, accepted or rejected, is not really at stake for either Tillich or Ellul. Nor do they honor the secular in a manner that would be consonant with biblical religion.

Neither dismayed nor fascinated by pluralism, biblical religion—Buber used to say—consists in the overcoming of religion, because it is world affirming. It calls for worlding the word—for the secular. Possibly now and then Tillich and Ellul would not disagree with this. But they still view basic issues in terms of an oppositional if not outright conflictual and—though mildly—dualistic dialectic. This is reverberated by such phrases as the vertical and the horizontal with Tillich or faith and religion with Ellul and is not altogether enfranchised from dubious connections to an irrepressibly sacred canopy. An enfranchised dialectic is a dialectic not of opposites but of *otherness,* in the light of which finite and infinite are locked into one another, and the infinite is not the negation of the finite but its denegation.

Language and Rorty's Blind Spot

Unlike Tillich's and Ellul's, Richard Rorty's approach to the secular is not only strikingly forthright, it also exhibits a significant peculiarity. It couples the secular with humility, not with the religious. Humility is, moreover, stripped of any religious connotation. It would even preempt religion. Oddly enough, what then suddenly dawns upon us is of even greater importance. By departing from traditional religious modalities of thought, Rorty equally departs from its classic philosophical anchorage: dealing with humility. Aristotle does not even consider it a virtue. It wears out on you even before you think of wearing it.[21] In contrast to self-esteem, which is not a vice either, it does not consist in estimating oneself as compared with others; it consists in so pairing oneself in relation to others as not to overrate or underrate them any more than oneself. It consists not in the practice of a particular quality but in the practice of that which has no quality of its own and through which one hangs on the mercy of others, of the other—as does anyone who, endowed with speech, is ipso facto spoken for, at the price of one's own self, should that be required for the sake of others. Even stripped of all religious connotations, humility still, and perhaps all the more emphatically, belongs to a lexicon associated with the notion of a word become flesh and its corresponding call for the worlding of this very word.

Given the parameters of Rorty's commitment to a deconstructive reassessment of our intellectual heritage, it is worth noting that humility, held at bay by metaphysics, has never swerved from bolstering the christological turn of Western rhetoric—provided that the figurative sense of "christological" is not here obliterated but underscored by the literal; or, again, provided that the literal is subsumed under the figurative. The secular is no substitute for the religious.

Rorty goes even further. Precisely because it is no substitute for the religious, the secular reaffirms the traditional view according to which the relation between faith and the world is not and cannot be exhausted by the religious. To be sure, in this traditional view, the secular is tied in with and implements the humility of the word become flesh. It does not stand for the humiliation of the world any more than it does with Rorty, for whom, moreover, the secular has radically broken away from the religious, or so he would have it seem.

Rorty has no truck with the religious, and when he says secular, he means secular, even with a vengeance. He does not hesitate, and he even repudiates each and every subtle substitute for religion advocated by modernity, such as philosophy.[22] Modernity, he points out, had us go from theology as queen of the sciences to science as the founding science of all sciences. Its ambition was no different: it aims at viewing, whether the world or the human predicament, from a God's-eye view, or any substitute thereof.

In his critique of the essentialist ontotheistic tradition of Western thought, Rorty's neo-pragmatist program may at times resemble Derrida's method of deconstruction. Or rather it would do so if the latter were pursued to the bitter end—whence his friendly fire–like barbs against Derrida, not to mention the even stricter reservations he formulates about Heidegger. Deconstruction is, for Rorty, only bound to abort if it remains obsessed with the primal world of some final vocabulary, with truth or objectivity—in other words, with contempt for this world and with its "salvation" rather than its transformation. Not contemplation from some God's-eye view but the screening of the choices laid before us is the order of the day. "[W]e already have," he writes, "as much theory as we need, and . . . what we need now are concrete utopias, and concrete proposals about how to get to those utopias from where we are now."[23] The only thing that counts consists in clarifying the ideas today's men and women have on those issues that divide them.[24] It is summed up in what, with Milan Kundera, he calls a *democratic utopia*. That is: "an imaginary future society where no one dreams of believing that God, or truth, or the Nature of things is on one's side. In this utopia, . . . in this community, there would be nothing that looked even remotely like a state religion or a state philosophy."[25]

Abrupt and challenging as this description of a democratic utopia is in its vindication of the secular, it remains shy of the concluding and even more radical description of the New Jerusalem (Revelation 21): it contains no temple—no religion of any kind, earthly or heavenly, much less a state philosophy or ideology of "final solution" or of any final vocabulary of some final religion. Why? Because no language being foreign to another, no religion is, either. What ideologically separates one from another does not overshadow or extenuate what they have in common: the secular.

5

The Secular and the Deregulation of Religion

This great distinction [between the nature
and limits of church power and secular power]
is the basis for tranquillity among all peoples:
it is a distinction funded not only by religion but
also by reason as well as by nature, each of them
demanding never to confuse things that in fact
are separate and can only subsist so far as they
are kept separate.

—Montesquieu, *Considérations sur les causes de la grandeur des Romains et de leur décadence*

There is no religion either in Saint Thomas More's Utopia. Nothing would be gained by replacing one religion with another. Being neither religious nor secular, More's utopia lies beyond such cleavage. It does not replace one holier-than-thou ideology of the good life and its final vocabulary with another, perhaps softer but equally noxious, ideological version of a similarly final solution. In other words, no island is merely an island, exclusively governed whether by so-called fundamentalists or by self-styled secularists. Utopia is a challenge to both. Horrifying both of them, it stands or falls as though it were "One nation under God." This phrase is as secular as it is religious. Besides establishing no religion, it warns the nation against the imperialistic pretense of one ultimate and final nation.

In a laconic comment he made a few decades ago about Christian churches in the modern period, Raymond Aron was pointing out how, after ceaseless upon interminable feuds, they had finally grown tired of killing one another in the name of one and the same God. What they bequeathed then was a novel idea: tolerance. But it is not tolerance among European nations only. To the rest of the world, they bequeathed the hope of a better world, of the best possible world. How could they mean to speak for all the other religions? Did they not, instead of speaking for them, simply acknowledge that through each other as well as through the other religions, each in its own right, they were spoken for? Or else they were blandly sawing the branch on which they were sitting. Or were they? Aron refrains from any hint that such attitudinal change on the part of the churches corresponds to some kind of loss of nerve. What counts, for us, lies elsewhere.

Between Theocracy and Anarchy: From the Sacred to Utopia

Consider the shift from Thomas Aquinas's beatific vision of God in heaven to Calvin's view of the future as hanging on the here-and-now of one's concomitant commitment to God and involvement in the world. Even rather than lying elsewhere, what counts lies here and now. What counts is actually the link Aron sets between church and utopia. In Rorty's terminology, what counts here is the "redescription" of a previous redescription of the Christian faith, in the light of which the self is no longer centered "by virtue of a common essence" but by reason of the fact that, since Adam left the Garden of Eden, now "personhood . . . is . . . a matter of decision rather than knowledge, an acceptance of another being into fellowship rather than a recognition of a common essence."[1] To use a word much in vogue in these days of identity crisis, personhood does not grow on commonalities. It happens upon you as you respond to the call of solidarity.[2]

Utopia and democracy thus collapse into one another, pushing one another's frontiers, further broadening the horizon of the least and yet most utopically concrete expression of democracy—namely, solidarity. It encompasses under the same purview not what we have so much as what we do not have in common. Where respect for the other is lacking, there is no solidarity, either. Sneering at democracy, Nietzsche can still be heard, saying, it "is Christianity made natural." Rorty's rebuke is all the more telling for the footnote he appends to it, writing: "Take away the sneer and he was right."[3] And, doubtless, Nietzsche was right—even more so if, instead of *natural*, he had said *secular*. Nietzsche's sentence flies in the face of Tillich's contention to the effect that, with Christianity, religion is cut loose from its anchorage in nature. Each in his own way views the religious as forming a pair with the natural. Neither of them quite allows for it to connect, even connive, with the secular, that is, where we happen to be. Where else can we start from if not from where we are? For all his fondness for the secular, Rorty's answer could be misleading.

A democratic utopia, Rorty contends, does not rest on nationalizing, as it were, the human self but on privatizing it. (Thinking of the model of humanitarian interference, I should have preferred he had said: on interfering with it through language, the home of the homeless.) It is in league with the concomitant assertion of freedom, of security (or well-being as the dialectic twin of being just, even as goods are of the good), and, last but not least, of solidarity. He does not mind taking a risk and adds that a democratic utopia is in league with "ethnocentrism." But he means nothing like ethnicism or ethnicity. What he means is a body politic geared to creating "a more expansive sense of solidarity than we presently have" rather than merely recognizing "such a solidarity, as something that exists antecedently to our own recognition of it." Otherwise, we should leave ourselves open to Nietzsche's insinuation that the end of religion and metaphysics should mean "the end of our attempts not to be cruel."[4] In case we still miss the point, Rorty adds that "what takes the curse off this ethnocentrism is not that the largest such group is 'humanity,' or 'all rational beings.'" He insists, "No one . . . can make that identification." What takes the curse off this ethnocentrism is, "rather, that it is the ethnocentrism of a 'we' ('we liberals') which is dedicated to enlarging itself, to creating an ever larger and more variegated ethnos. It is the 'we' of the people who have been brought up to distrust ethnocentrism."[5]

Or else where can we start if not from where we are? A democratic utopia is no flight into another world. Relentless, it can cope only with the world as it is. Borrowing Reinhold Niebuhr's famous phrase, a democratic utopia is a method of finding approximate solutions for insoluble problems. It is a method funded by the notion that the moral progress we are capable of, as human beings, is itself dependent on repentance and is at the same time an acknowledgment of our sinfulness, just as it is meant to anticipate the perfection we are supposed to reflect by virtue of our being created in the image of God. Can I believe in God unless I confess my unbelief? It is not that I expect Rorty to nod any kind of approval here. Suffice it for him to acknowledge that "[s]imply by being human we do not have a common bond. For all we share with all other humans is the same thing we share with all other animals—the ability to feel pain."[6] Whether we share the same ultimate vocabulary is beside the point in a democratic utopia. Where we stand is precisely at the point where you are in pain—even as the parable of the Good Samaritan also makes clear, not to mention the parable of the Last Judgment.[7]

We all have different ultimate vocabularies, and these are carried on with their respective hosts of questions. The point Rorty makes is that "distinguishing these questions makes it possible to distinguish public from private questions, questions about pain from questions about the point of human life." This even makes it possible to distinguish "the domain of the liberal from the domain of the ironist. In a more important way, however, distinguishing these questions makes it possible for a single person to be both a liberal and an ironist."[8] Why not? After all, as incongruous as the rapprochement may be, why should a stance like this not remind us of Luther's understanding of the believer as being at once justified and sinful? Would that be because—it is no secret—Rorty does not much like Luther? But this kind of Luther—who knows? Rorty might even appreciate him.

At any rate, compare Rorty's notion of democratic utopia as consisting in ethnocentrism subverting itself and Luther's notion of faith as the subversion of religion. What else does one hear but an echo of the biblical contention that faith consists in religion overcoming religion, even as the encompassing overcomes the sum total of its parts, or even as truth lies beyond and likewise overcomes the opposition of the One and the Many? Truth no more than faith makes you an enlisted person; it makes you free. As Karl Mannheim points out in another context, should there be "only one Truth, it is bound to be more comprehensive than any one human being or any other party could grasp."[9]

We must leap before we look. Where we start from is where we stand—not where we come from but where we must bifurcate, and turn the page. We do not know where to start from unless we turn the page. How does one do it? Here is John Cotton's answer.

Speaking from where he stood, at the dawn of the American Commonwealth, this is what Cotton wrote, and it remains relevant yet to this day: "It is necessary that all power on earth be limited, Church power or other. . . . It is counted [by some] a matter of danger to the state to limit Prerogatives; but it is a further danger not to have them limited. . . . And it is meet that magistrates in the Commonwealth and officers in the Churches should desire to know the utmost bounds of their own power."[10] No commonwealth is worth the venture unless it both demands and complies with its paramount prospect. And this is a prospect that aims at desacralizing every seat of power—priestly or ideological, religious or metaphysical.[11] It is a prospect from which no one can swerve, if morality is to hinge on language and if linguistic interference is to be the vector, whether of communication or of community, that is, of a ceaseless, permanent commutation of power; or again if, as Rorty himself puts it, morality is to be a matter of vocabulary, since "languages are historical contingencies rather than attempts to capture the true shape of the world or the self"; and, finally, if to "stand unflinchingly for one's moral convictions is a matter of identifying oneself with such a contingency."[12]

The Two Bodies of the Christ

Desacralization and secularization are the twin aspects of one and the same process stemming from the biblical option for the primacy of language over nature and history as receptacle of faith—a purely nominal receptacle, given the thoroughgoing metaphoricity of language. Speaking is believing. Yet even as language dodges the idol, it also turns God into an idol as soon as God is worshipped and is identified with this or that. It has no end, either. Nothing to which language might refer lies outside its purview. For thus being wholly contingent, it points to the ultimate all the more—to that of which our life is the basic experience, once and for all. In this light, desacralization and secularization overlap and are interchangeable. They are combined in the same process, through which religion is freed from its fetters in nature or history, while the secular is retrieved from the status to which it is reduced by being identified with the profane. And if, as Tillich contends, the Christian tradition results in denaturing religion, it does not lead to the denaturing of nature but restores it to the natural (Bultmann). God need no longer be the personification of either a natural or a historical process.

Precisely what puts an end to such pretensions is in the biblical tradition the notion of covenant—linguistic, mind you, if at all real. It is not that it denies natural or historical process. It keeps them honest, so to speak, assigning to each the rank to which it belongs. Correspondingly, the covenant encompasses all that is—creation as a whole and humankind in particular.

But this is a notion that would also harbor some degree of suspicion to which it would succumb if it were not sheltered by the suggestion that a covenant is equally a matter of convenience between two parties: it must be renewed—time and again, constantly. Every covenant is a new covenant each time it is the landmark of a story turned into a scenario—a story of the otherworld turned into the scenario for a new world, a new creation, a new being. It is a new language for which God is not a God who is so much as a God who comes, and not a God who comes first but who comes down.

In the Old Testament, the Promised Land symbolizes salvation. It hangs on the concretion, not on the deferral, of salvation to the otherworld. There is a territorial dimension to it.[13] But we should not be misled. This Land is no pretext for carving out some national piece of real estate, the rights to which would be implemented or controlled by ties of mere blood and soil. The Promised Land is emblematic of another kind of right—the right to the earth, to a place in the sun for anyone born to the world, whether descending from Abraham or by way of any other lineage.[14]

In the New Testament, salvation deals with being gathered together to the body of Christ, an emblem of the new world order inasmuch as, in Christ, there is neither Greek nor Jew, neither master nor slave, neither male nor female—and neither God nor "man." For neither God nor "man" but the Christ is now the measure of all things. And this is the Christ who does not begin his ministry by preaching salvation in some life after death or eternal life in some world beyond this world. He begins by proclaiming the kingdom of God. He repeals the sacral paradigm of religion.

Jesus's proclamation refers to another paradigm to which the biblical tradition adheres. The God that saves is also the maker of all things and beings, even as the God that liberates Israel from bondage in Egypt is also the creator of heaven and earth, through the fulfillment of which on the seventh day the whole world is hallowed. It becomes a stage on which the glory of God, God's reign, is at stake. God would even rely on us. But we would rather return the compliment and let the God that reigns slide over into a God that saves, allowing us to pile up excuses for our shortcomings and to make amends for them time and again, hoping God will be all in all in the end.

Even so, God's covenant is never the exclusivity of any one people, or else that very people would not be people of God. Nor is the covenant the exclusivity of those who, gathered together in view of worlding the word, are gathered into the body of Christ, the word become flesh. It is not physical pain that likens human beings to one another; it does not generate solidarity beyond the family, or the clan, or the tribe, or the race. Suffering does. What we have in common is that, so long as being human is pending on a human being, this human being suffers from being human—as do the lame and the blind who, together with the poor and hoping against hope, hope nevertheless to be made whole again and reconciled with themselves, to be saved. As pain is to suffering, so salvation is to the kingdom of God. Pain can be located. The kingdom is neither here nor there. This is a kingdom that—with Jesus and the prophets before him—is told and brought about only to the extent that, speaking of it, we are spoken for. It is the ultimate parable of language. And as Jesus's own disciples admit, it is more difficult to understand than the language of pain, or of salvation.[15] One question, already adumbrated by the Gospels, will subsequently sum up this view of the human predicament: "What must I do to be saved?" or its more philosophical counterpart, "Why does God become man?"

The question will haunt the Western ethos as well as its religious consciousness. Overlapping the expectation of the kingdom, the quest of salvation will soon override the eschatic scope of faith. Salvation will even obsess metaphysics, rhetoric and the necessitarianism of its substantialist categories notwithstanding. Even so, Western culture never loses sight of the eschatological dimension of salvation and its resolution through the kingdom of God. Always in quest of a "true country" (Calvin), it continues to look forward to the Promised Land, to the New Jerusalem—or, for that matter, a new commonwealth. This is a commonwealth in which, as already suggested by quoting John Cotton, churches, not to speak of the church, are *only* meant to share responsibility in joint efforts aimed at restructuring the social reality. And because this is an eminently civic responsibility, churches can only share in it, as they must, if, conforming to the biblical understanding of the relation between the religious and the secular, they would heed its explicitly paradigmatic mandate to hallow this world.[16]

But what this means is not only that the biblical paradigm of religion is utopian but also that its utopianism assigns religion to an ancillary role, if only because religion must always overcome itself. This also means that such a paradigm is not restricted to the biblical tradition. If it is at work in Jerusalem, this utopian paradigm of religion paradoxically is also at work in Athens.[17] Admittedly, the flamboyant polytheism of the Greek cities stands in sharp contrast to the radical monotheism covenanting God and the chosen people. But it is a contrast between cities or the body politic on the one hand and a chosen people or the body of Christ on the other—metaphors of the relation between the human and the divine, regardless of how this relation is construed. On the Areopagus, whether God is one or many does not bother Paul.[18] This difference is not what counts, since, as Pascal will point out centuries later, it is only a matter of geography, or of how the divine, singular or plural, happens to be enshrined. But the divine is not to be reached by adding to it or subtracting from it.[19] It is closer to us than we are to each other or even to ourselves. More significantly, we are its entire "offspring," states Paul, who profiles the figure of the Athenians' body politic through that of the body of Christ yet without violating the integrity of either.

Paul's argument lies beyond the opposition of polytheism and monotheism, even beyond that of theism and atheism. The fact is that, whether the world worships one or many gods, it is full of gods. There is no worldview that does not somehow flatter itself on performing some "God's-eye view," as Rorty might say. The important thing is, for Paul, that because of the Christ-event or, differently put, because God is not God without the world, a world come of age need no longer be divinized, however subtly this is achieved. Through the Christ as worlding of the word become flesh, the world embodies a God emptied of Godself.[20] It is dedivinized. It is restored to its worldhood, its secularity. Moreover, through this figure of Christ—of anyone "raised from the dead," as Paul keeps affirming—every man or woman is likewise to be raised from the empty tomb enshrined by any worldview in the name of any God, through which human beings express how they are concerned, if not obsessed, with their salvation or, as the case may be, with their perfection.[21]

Beyond Pluralism and Fundamentalism: A Bridge over a River without Banks

For not being atheistic, biblical language is not that much theistic, either. It consists in dedivinizing the world. It is messianic, which is to say christological, rather than christocentric or ontotheistic, if such attributes still have any meaning. To be sure, with the New Testament, the measure of all things is Christ, the Lamb of God. This is a sacrificial emblem. But together with the wolf, this lamb is also the emblematic figure of ultimate peaceableness throughout the whole creation. An emblem of the other, utopic, dimension of the human predicament and as subversive as the sabbatical law, it subverts all preestablished, so-called harmony. The lamb and the wolf were already lying down together in the prophets' vision of messianic times. In early Christian iconography, the utopian hope they anticipate reverberates through stories of miraculous fishing, of water turned into wine, and of the lame that walk, the blind that see, the deaf that hear, the sick that are healed and, again, of the even more radical sharing of bread.

Notice that of the life situations to which we have just referred, none is really worth an ultimate concern that is not also concerned with the practicalities of life. Not the slightest wedge is driven between ultimate and penultimate concerns. We stand at the opposite end from the endless sighing of supernatural salvation, deferred until after life, and until well-being is actually eclipsed by some abstract being, and beings are eclipsed by speculations about being-itself.

Do we always need an umbrella of sorts, or a net of some kind or another? Do we still need crutches, or stopgaps? Put differently, what does it take for a symbol to be a symbol? Does it—and why must it—take more than what it is by itself? How could anything carry a symbolic charge if it were not already literally true by itself? Does bread need to turn into something else in order to symbolize the presence of Christ? What better symbol could there be of the body of Christ than bread that is real bread rather than a symbol of it, bread that is all the more symbolic for being real bread? And what is real bread if not that bread which, for all its simulating, dissimulates nothing of itself? However mystically or, for that matter, ontologically troped, even a simulacrum is never merely a simulacrum. It is harder to come by than one usually imagines. As illustrated by gods that die and are born again, their tomb is never empty, and the myth it yields, potent as it may be, is scarcely short of a theodicy. Yet soteric ontotheism will pick up this motif. And it will prolong it by further distinguishing flesh and spirit in an attempt to cope with—if not to explain, and explain away—evil and suffering through their eschatological sublation in heaven after Judgment Day.[22]

But even so, soteric ontotheism rests its case not on a tomb but on an empty tomb: no simulacrum is merely a simulacrum. There is nothing that can support the spirit save the flesh, and there is no point in looking for it in the body of Jesus if you do not find it in the body of Christ—originally as secular a body politic as one could hope for. And just this was nevertheless the body that was actually superseded by a totalizing mystical reality—namely, the church.[23] The ethic of faith gave way to a system—and so exclusive a system that without it there would be no salvation, so exclusive that its event could only result in a simulacrum. Through this, nothing happens but the futility of a faith that, because it has deprived the spirit of its anchorage in the flesh, has ultimately divested the religious of its own and only harbor in the secular—in an empty tomb.

Even shrunk into a religion of salvation, Christianity could never wholly renege this dimension, call it secular utopianism or utopic secularity, which is typical of its faith. It stems not from an analogical but from a tropological use of language, and just because of that, it can be denied or forgotten. It can be silenced. But it cannot be negated without being denegated. Should nothing but stones be left of it, it would still rise from them so long as it could raise up children to Abraham.[24] Most emblematic of this eschatic dimension of faith and the tropological use of language by which it is tested and attested is a triptych running through the biblical tradition. It consists of three propositions: there is no sacred enclosure in the Garden of Eden; there is no temple in the New Jerusalem, either; so also is the tomb empty. Summed up in one, they read: religion has no future except through the secular.

By making the transmission of faith dependent upon inherited institutions, the Christian tradition proved only that it could be forgetful of the fact that no transmission can occur that is not relayed by new institutions. Calvin was still aware of that when he issued his *Institutes of the Christian Religion* (and not "essence" and much less "the new essence," as centuries later some will continue to label their books). As every lawyer knows, all institutions, however long they may last, are necessarily headed for a change. They are secular. If they make sense, then they also make sense despite the religious context of their inauguration. And just this is what modernity sensed. Most conspicuously drawing a most spectacular benefit, it accepts the legacy but does not acknowledge the legator. Unscrupulous to the end, modernity lords it over until it finally is caught short of itself, when it reaches its ultimate resolution in the postmodern deregulation of thought—a deregulation, one must add, that is achieved only in the aftermath of an even broader deregulation—namely, the deregulation of religion.

Of course, this phrase "deregulation of religion" is not wholly innocent. It evokes a lingering recollection of the medieval distinction between the regular clergy on the one hand and the secular clergy on the other. In a more significant way, it is also meant to sharpen our conception as well as our perception of the secular *post mortem dei*. Even if Christianity had a privileged relationship to the secular, it no longer does so after the death of God. No religion now can boast of a mortgage on the secular: Christians must talk with Jews and both with Muslims and all of them with adepts of other religions. But they cannot do that unless they let their institutions undergo some radical mutation. What is at stake is not their integrity but their ability to enter and sustain a dialogue on the grounds of the only thing they have in common—the secular, the worldhood of a world common to all that come into it, and for whom "here is no abiding city."[25] Abraham leaves his birthplace and goes to God alone knows where. Ulysses returns to Ithaca and takes off again.

In the hierarchical sacral order of the world, a tower like the Tower of Babel is indeed intended to be symbolic of the city. But the story makes it clear: what is wrong with a vertical city is that it is not quite a city; it is only some kind of stopgap between the natural and the supernatural, between the profane and the sacred. Intent on making a name for themselves, the planners want to build "a tower with its top in the heavens," lest they should "be scattered abroad upon the face of the whole earth."[26] For them, being human is no challenge to the human being.

In contrast, consider once again the Garden of Eden. What marks it, in the absence of any sacral reminder, are the four rivers by which, far from being enclosed, it is *delimited*. Aside from what is immediately brought to mind and what reminds us of our dependence upon nature, a river is a challenge to human being: it is obviously there only in order to be traveled up or down or to be crossed. No wonder a ship has always been the symbol of the church, while religion has been identified with building bridges.[27] From one bank of a river to the other, a bridge brings together whomever nothing can separate, let alone oneself from one's own. Calling in question all that ranges from egotism and solipsism to tribalism and racism, it summons all human being to being human. It shifts the ground of our human condition from nature or history to human nature and destiny, to a *technē* of which language is the paramount modality.

Throughout, not only do we speak, not only are our lips muted into words; we are also spoken for. Language, spanning subject and object, human being and being human, is like a bridge thrown over a river without banks. And it is humanly made to the extent that, like a bridge, it is not found in nature; and yet, not unlike the natural bridge that a rainbow is, it is all the more the symbolic harbinger of a new covenant.[28] Funding everything except itself, language is not funded by anything outside itself unless, for want of bridging words and the word, it has fossilized or entombed itself, as would a mere landmark of the past. It does not set one thing off from another. Nor does it draw a line between *them* and *us*.[29] Likewise, instead of drawing a line between the religious and the secular, it switches them on to one another.

By comparison, consider the altar rail. A hangover from the dualism of the sacred and the profane, it still refers God to the telluric primacy of sacred space. As impressive as this primacy of space over time may be visually, it is a tribute to a sacral order of things; at the expense of their expressivity, it is forgetful of language. It forgets that, from a biblical standpoint, not nature but language is the *space* of creation. Only through language is nature and, a fortiori, human nature conscious of itself, even as distance is a matter of time. And time deals not with that which has been, as the sacralization of space does,[30] but with that which is and is only because, even in the language of myth, it happens once upon a time. Because once upon a time, language is itself a parable—not so much a story as a scenario. And, as with Jesus, a parable inaugurates a shift from one form of the religious paradigm to another as well as from the sacral to the utopic paradigm of religion—even ultimately to a new type of religiosity.

No religion is ever immune from the temptation of sacralizing itself. As recalled earlier, again and again, it lies in overcoming itself. This is acknowledged even by so conservative a scholar as Eliade. In an age that revels in playing one religion against another, in calling for their disintegration while allowing for all manners of crispation in their usurpative claims of legitimacy in a world beyond the pale of their once-valid purview; in an age that revels in wallowing through sundry fads of do-it-yourself rearrangements of the religious landscape, Eliade himself writes that, nevertheless, "it is not excluded that the attraction of myths and symbols, the obsession with the exotic, the primitive, the archaic, the encounter with 'Others' and all the ambivalent feelings they imply,—it is not excluded that some day all this will appear to be *a new type of religiosity*" (emphasis mine).[31]

But do we ever learn anything from religion?

In view of a new type of religiosity, Abraham leaves his place of birth and Israel, the land of slavery. And in the same passion of faith, the early Christians claim for themselves no distinction "from the rest of humanity either in locality or in speech or in customs. For they do not dwell off somewhere in cities of their own, neither do they use some different language, nor do they practice an extraordinary style of life. . . . But while they dwell in cities of Greeks and Barbarians as the lot of each is cast, . . . the constitution of their citizenship is nevertheless quite amazing and admittedly paradoxical. They dwell in their own countries, but only as sojourners. . . . Every foreign country is a fatherland to them, and every fatherland is a foreign country."[32] Not the least trace of a discrimination between them and us here, nothing harks back, be it in a monistic or a pluralistic mood, to the conflictual dialectic of identity and difference or its "negative," complementarity. Moreover, the idealism if not the absolutism implied by the latter is replaced with the more practical, even pragmatic, notion of compatibility, which implies otherness so far as the opposition of us and them has given way to the binary—though not dualistic—dialectic of I and Thou and, to repeat, the logic of being to the "logos," or christic logic, of language.

God is a God who speaks. The God who is the maker of all does not come up with a religion but makes a new thing, a world for the sake of which solidarity with creation as a whole, including the secular, cancels any sacredness attached to rituals and their concatenation of beings into bondage to one another. Only this God who speaks is at an equal distance from all creatures. But it is only through *homo loquens* that this God is at an equal distance from all that is, as Augustine contends in one of his own most imaginative parables of language. Asked who created them, every creature refers or, better still, defers the question to another, higher creature and so on until *homo loquens* is called upon. He breaks the chain of pluses and minuses, of more and less, of this and that, of the One and the Many. Restored each to its respective autonomy, all creatures are creatures of God. Through them the creation as a whole is hallowed, and by the same token, in league with all that is, humanized is that which above all is alien to itself, the human.[33]

Because the human is an unfinished task (Saint Thomas), being human can alone surpass the human being (Pascal). Such humanizing of the human can be no tribal, exclusivist business. It calls for solidarity, be it at the cost of secularity, or at the cost of a utopia. Today's legitimization of humanitarian interference, of human rights and the like, not to mention technology—all these phenomena deal a fatal blow not only to overt religious fundamentalism but also to its covert versions under the guise either of pluralism or of multiculturalism. If religion is the substance of culture, religion cannot lag behind culture unless it becomes a fossil. In a technological civilization, it cannot afford to forgo a radical mutation if it must anticipate the new type of religiosity foreseen even by Eliade. Ghettoized and shorn of a cultural setting, it can only turn into or feed an ideology, compensating for its lost relevance by an ever more exacerbated fundamentalism, whether religious or political. Even so-called cultural differences—honorable as they may be—need at least to be called into question, supposing they are not belied by the only thing all cultures, like all religions, have in common: the secular.

Cultural pluralism results in a conundrum if, in order to encompass religion as its form, it is not iconoclastic—as it must be of regressive cultural identities, to be sure, but no more than, to begin with, it must be of itself. Downgrading the secular by downsizing secularity to secularism, it must keep above all from sacralizing itself—a task no less and actually more demanding than it was of religious monism.

With the secular, theology recovers its integrity and becomes at last *autonomous*. Like *nomos*, which is to be distinguished from *physis*, it belongs to the sphere of *logos*, of language, and being therefore somewhat arbitrary, it is at one and the same time free from and tempted by theonomy and heteronomy. Anarchy and theocracy have the same root—the rootlessness of faith, as shown by Abraham, the iconoclast and father of faith.

But unlike the Greek iconoclast Prometheus, Abraham is no hero. Abraham, who as a youth smashes his father's idols, is so religious that he is ready and willing to sacrifice his own son, until God stops him. Atavistic or whatever the anthropological explanation, it takes God to debunk religion. And this God is the God who speaks and the thing happens, the word becomes flesh and is worlded once and for all, secular and religious as well, with no more a sacred spot in the Garden of Eden than a temple in the New Jerusalem.

6

Worlding the Word

Incarnation and the Otherness of Time

The Lord [Eternal] is my shepherd, I lack nothing.

—Psalm 23

I am the first and the last, the living One. I was dead; and behold, I am alive for evermore.

—Revelation 1:18

Joseph called the name of the first-born Manasseh. "For," he said, "God has made me forget all my hardships and all my father's house."

—Genesis 41:51

There is no time when time was not. Nor would anything everlasting last even an instant. Being is timing. Given time, I lack nothing. *Time is a gift*—a trace in the sand, a deposition of which there is no recollection except through fictions of language. Like sand lying in the sun and erased by wind or sea, memory, lying in language, lies in and—hoping against hope—is erased by the expectation of a language through which nothing happens that is not without precedent: a new being and a new heaven as well as a new earth, once and for all.

If there is a text that really seems "timeless," that seemingly acquires a no less timeless patina, it is the passage in *Confessions* where Saint

Augustine tackles the most banal of conversation topics—time: what is it? He lets go of the handrail and indulges a remark as simple as it is sublime: "I know well enough what it is, provided that nobody asks me; but if I am asked what it is and try to explain, I am baffled."[1] Given time, nothing so frustrates knowledge as does knowledge, or memory as does memory. Knowledge is, for Augustine, bound up with memory, and memory with knowledge, and both seem to hang on time. But time, littering or scattered about on their interface, is less a negation of knowledge than a denegation of memory. One thing is to remember or to know. Another is to have faith. And, no doubt, having faith is like having time. They hang on one another. You cannot have anything on faith unless you have it on time, even as the time you have you can only have on faith. And what is the use of time if not to wear faith, especially if, moreover, faith itself consists not of drawing God out of forgetfulness but of *timing* God? Timing God is more than simply reminiscing God, just as knowledge is more than a vestige of time, just as memory is no shortening of time but a desire for time and its fullness, its timeliness rather than its timelessness.

No more so than knowledge is memory timeless. Or else it would go blind—not only blind but also oblivious of the fact that it expresses as much as it represses, or it impresses as much as it oppresses. It lingers on only because, whether they be oppressed or repressed, all leftovers alike have in the process been marginalized by history and denied their right to mark the calendar of time. Even belying time, history is the strong man's story: it repeats itself—as genocide subsequently reminds us.

Dated—Not Outdated: Timing the Eternal

Subject to oblivion or remembrance, no genocide is unique unless all are. Led by rulers who would not exonerate themselves from the least person's death, a genocide will soon be forgotten, especially if such rulers, "undefeated" on the world stage, continue to steal the geopolitical show. Remembered only by its victims, sooner or later, a genocide is "recycled" by history— and the euphemism is not innocent: unless a genocide is forgiven rather than merely forgotten, history can only repeat itself. Always mangled by impenitent history, memory had better be left in the hands of those victims who are denied the "right" to forgive. They alone can forgive and forget.

Time does not repeat itself. It can only be given—or forgiven. No wonder time is the time of God's patience, of God's passion for humans, through whom God "forgets" himself, as does a mother through her child. And just as a child is timing a mother's passion, so also are humans timing God's passion for all that is, for the world, through which, forgetting Godself in time, God lies in timing a passion. It is a passion for time fulfilled and yet rehearsed time and again. Or, for that matter, time is "redeemed"[2] once and for all. Or else knowledge or morality would have no past, and memory, bereft of a present in which it invested itself, would have no future through which it could forget itself—for the time being.

Indeed, so long as it is caught between a past already gone and a future that is not yet, time is only present once and for all. It lasts, but only as would a bridge spanning a river without banks. It lasts, but only as does that which cannot be measured, like a masterpiece that, though dated, is never outdated. It bodies forth, even as the word becomes flesh when the time comes. Time is *appointment,* though not in the manner of this or that which happened once upon a time, but of that which happens once and for all. For that same reason it is also *dis-appointment.* Or else it would be reduced to what is no longer, or to what is not yet. It would be reduced to chronology, to arithmosophy, even to meteorology. It would even be eclipsed by as many figures of time as it is disfigured by, were it not for that property of time to reconfigure itself, to redeem and yet be redeemed, and pass yet without passing itself by: the only thing that outlives time is outlived time—a contradiction if not the very dis-appointment of time by itself.

Still, what is time? In French, the same word, *temps,* designates both time and the weather; while in English, "time," at one and the same time, designates the time, the hour, and the number. Somehow time can be and is all that. Time is accordingly summoned and screened each time through a different logic, another grammar of time than that of a present caught between a past and a future and their respective satellites. Regardless of how significant that may be, time itself is a grab-bag word. It is a word for which nothing is that is off-limits, a word that countenances nothing it does not delimit—and even is itself delimited by what it countenances. It outwits all grammar, as does an exception that confirms the rule, or as do past, present, and future when they clear a way for time and at the same time numb its very timing. The problem is that the grammar of time is not reducible to words, much less to those that *tell* time. Time is not a matter of telling but of timing. Telling is linear; timing is binary.[3]

Take, for example, the chronicles of the kings of Israel. As behooves kings, they succeed one upon the other, the good upon the less good, like the lean cows upon the fat cows. But does that justify looking at time only under the aspect of a succession? Instead of a linear sequence, eventually zigzagging to the point of caricature, must we not view it as unfolding, not one more, but a new and more radical grammar of time?

It is too bad if this displeases conventional ideas, but biblical time is, at one and the same time, binary and alternative rather than linear and successive. Pointing to an "either/or," it is "accomplished" or "unaccomplished," past on the one hand and future on the other, perfect on the one hand and, accordingly, imperfect on the other. In keeping with the biblical ear, only that lasts which can and must change and does change. And only that changes which has no past. Time that passes has no past. Just as when the creation happens, nothing happens that had already happened before or that ever will happen, in the new creation, after God has made everything from new.[4] The apparent dialectic of identity and difference notwithstanding, the quest for sameness and the alienation it postulates give way to the primacy of otherness of which solidarity is the avant-garde, the premise, the prolepsis.

Unlike space that is seen, time is heard. Whatever space brings together, it confines and territorializes, including religion. Time delimits and deterritorializes even religion, switching it from one worlding of the word to another, from Israel to the nations. Space diversifies and, distending us from one another, "alienates" us. Time relates: it extends the self to that from which it is most remote—namely, the alien, the stranger—so that the self, hosting that which is alien to itself, is gathered to itself and, related to itself, is related to the other. Time secularizes what space sacralizes. Space collects: it maps out. As does the legend that helps to read a map, time recollects: it interprets, and therefore it bets on a hermeneutic principle that is essentially proleptic so far as there is no time when time is not. Nor is there a time when time does not happen and, from beginning to end, last once and for all, world without end. Now. Past and future, like memory and hope, fused together, are but a fiction of time. That is, they tell a time that, having no past so long as it passes, need not happen unless it happens once and for all. The cacophony gives way before the creation; there is a time for the heavens and a time for the earth; there is a time for everything. From now on there is, above all and whatever the regime, a time for the human and a time for God, more especially since God is not merely any God of time.

Worlding the Word | 107

No doubt, Saint Augustine is fascinated by all that: he invents autobiography, and immediately time rather than matter looms up on the horizon of being as principle of individuation, the tracing of which he outlines by writing not dialogues à la Plato but soliloquies. (I do not say monologues.) Speaking with himself as though he spoke to another, Augustine realizes he cannot do so unless he takes or gives himself time. And he cannot have time unless that other—God or himself—is not demeaned into the status of a hostage or a ventriloquist. Man or woman, no human is ever as near to God as when one is human, fully all too human. This is so for the simple reason that God is then not only different from all that is but can only defer to that which is human—to that than which God is radically other. And God is therefore totally other even though in what we call an experience of God, we have the experience of God's absence no less than of God's presence. At Bethel, quite appropriately, only a heap of stones marks Jacob's encounter with God, present or absent, neither present nor absent.[5] The God who speaks to us is not a God who is now present, now absent, but a God who is revealed as radically other. The same thing holds in comparing time and eternity, or a man and a woman who have access to themselves only through their respective other.[6]

We do not keep time but its memory, at best harking both of them back to one another. And switching time into memory, we tell time, but each time we do so we actually turn time not so much into memory as into story. It is a story told again and again from one generation to the next, regardless of how much of a make-believe the recasting of roles turns out to be: the die is already cast. Turned into story, memory is self-serving. It had better be forgotten. But if, instead, memory is switched back to time, the story—of which memory is but the legend—gives way to a scenario whose impromptu enactment provides memory with a new script. In the absence of any prior script, nothing is played out in advance. No memory belongs to us unless, through our action, it can belong to others yet without their being compelled into it. Memory is singular only if it can be universalized. On this hangs the difference between story and scenario.

Turning the exodus from Egypt from a story to a scenario, Genesis universalizes the destiny as well as the ancestry of the children of Israel. Because the same happens with the incarnation, I call scenario that which, for the time being and regardless of whatever role we should play in this world, confronts us with a brand new mandate. It is an obligation, toward oneself as well as other people—an obligation toward the other. Should this even result in a zero-sum operation, time would be a mandate[7]—and not only money.

Time is not only money, even though by reason of the very terms of this encounter with the other in the stream of time is woven a demand of which I am at once creditor and debtor—creditor and yet (*et tamen*) debtor, debtor *et tamen* creditor.[8] In contrast with the ineluctable, historicist dualism of "already/not yet," the dialectic prompted by an *et tamen* approach is binary: mounting a genuine challenge to freedom, it stems from that radically *eschatic*[9] option thanks to which the biblical tradition resists the lure of dualism and is equally kept from sinking into the no less false if fascinating alternative of monism.

The fact is that between "accomplished" and "unaccomplished," those two tenses known to Hebrew, the present is no line of demarcation: the present is coeval with both that which is to pass and that which is to come, the ephemeral and the everlasting. It only lasts once and for all. Destiny is what happens when time suffers neither addition nor subtraction, and all suspicion of pointillism or of hypostatized sameness is by the same token disavowed. The present is no part of a process likened to the serpent that bites its own tail (cyclical time blending with nature). Nor is it, in a linear view of time, some rider to an arrow of time that might on occasion be pulled back into the genealogy of a trace—or more simply of a race, be it tribal, national, or cultural. Time is never so linear as to retract into so timeless a story that it would outlast itself, as though it had the last word. Words never have the last word.

Stories that make that kind of claim are of two kinds. Based on the Hebraic course of the world are those that finally stumble upon the apocalyptic view of life. On the other, Hellenistic, side of the spectrum are stories according to which, in search of the last word, of the ultimate revelation, one starts from nature and arrives at Gnosticism and is initiated into ultimate knowledge. Although apocalypse and Gnosticism, those twin temptations, have not ceased to torment Christianity, it has mostly learned how to keep clear of them, for two reasons. On the one hand, time that comes to an end (apocalypse)[10] finally is time that, deprived of actuality, of destiny, is reduced to sheer chronology. Or it would be so reduced, were it not for the fact that even so, and however literally construed, chronology, not unlike destiny, consists in a symbolic reconstruction of time insofar as, for example, events are dated from the year in which this or that king began to reign. On the other hand, the more knowledge is based on evidence, the more it calls for the knower's assent and even the consent of the collectivity. No knowledge is final and can pretend to be only if (as with Gnosticism) time were to suspend its flight and become frozen time. Knowing, then, amounts to blurring the boundary between believing and doubting, between the temporal and the eternal. It amounts to blurring the miracle by turning itself into the miracle of miracles—a miracle that denies itself. Believing is no more miraculous than knowing. Otherwise, knowledge would be to faith as image would be to the word, able no longer even to tell a tale. As being is to language, so also are knowing and believing an equivalent price tag to that which nevertheless is priceless, a revelation so final as to rest on the transitoriness of any language, be it that of faith.

Whether through believing or through knowing, nothing is ever revealed to anyone who, lacking nothing, much less God, does not lack oneself either and stands revealed to oneself. This depends neither on emptying God of Godself or the self of itself nor on a self lacking nothing but itself or God. This depends on a self enabled through language to time with its own self by way of another. Timing with oneself is timing with other people—with that which is radically other. Time is otherness. It is a metaphor of language.

Trailed on by nature or history, time is blown out and flattened to a trace or a story. In contrast, a scenario is hatched when time, intrigued with language, is inspirited by it. Sublating rather than merely relating temporality, language parses time and rather than turning it into memory puts it into words. Not unlike the verb in a phrase, it shepherds time, temporalizing that which happens once and for all, from creation to fulfillment by way of incarnation. To the psalmist who declares "The Everlasting One is my shepherd" echoes the Christ who says "I am the good shepherd."[11]

They said of Saint Augustine that he invented the philosophy of history. And they hastened to dull the very heart of his thought: the incarnation. In spite of Greek mythology and its plethora of personified gods, Augustine (who has himself shown an eager taste for all the available beliefs and chiefly wandered from Manichaeism to Neoplatonism)—Augustine realizes that myth does in fact provide everything one could desire, except for incarnation. Incarnation means that time is not only succession, smooth, coherent, and so solid in its continuity as to be persuasive; it is also what reminds us that nothing lasts that does not last for the last time. Time is as much disrupted as it seems continuous. Although it moves now with small steps and now by big leaps forward, it has no beginning and no end. It is probed only by that which, no longer being what it was, is at the same time that which it is not—probed only by that which is eternal. No biological phenomenon, the word become flesh lies between a virgin birth and an empty tomb.

With Augustine, from cosmology or genealogy (physical time), time is switched on language, through which it sounds, on the one hand, like chronology (historical) and, on the other, like eschatology. "For we know, O Lord," he writes, "that the extent to which something once was, but no longer is, is the measure of its death; and the extent to which something once was not, but now is, is the measure of its beginning. Your Word, then, in no degree gives place to anything or takes the place of anything, because it is truly immortal and eternal. Therefore it is by a Word co-eternal with yourself that you say all that you say; you say all at one and the same time, yet you say all eternally; and it is by this Word that all things are made which you say are to be made. You create them by your Word alone and in no other way. Yet the things which you create by your Word do not all come into being at one and the same time, nor are they eternal."[12]

Augustine does not content himself with psychologizing time and telling its inner story. For him time is not a mere narrative. It is above all relation. Nor does he satisfy himself with historicizing time. He secularizes it and thus refers us to the *saeculum* with all the connotations evinced by this term: temporal (*siècle*)[13] as well as spatial (world), as in the oxymoron-like "world without end." Developing all this, Augustine does it, however, by articulating the dialectic of the city of God and the earthly city in such a way that—as they must—fullness of time and incarnation hang on one another.

Put differently: this introvert that was Saint Augustine is also someone who thinks in terms of the church. And who cannot fully discuss the incarnation without appointing it to the secularization of time, whether by desacralizing nature ("natural man" is reproved simply because no one could be natural except by grace) or, for the same reasons, by defatalizing history? More than a philosophy of history, what Augustine stresses is a theology of time, of the seventh day, when addressing God he writes, the day is "without evening and the sun shall not set upon it, for you have sanctified and

Worlding the Word | 111

willed that it shall last for ever." Still addressing God, he adds, "Although your eternal repose was unbroken by the act of creation, nevertheless, after all your works were done and you had seen that they were very good, you rested on the seventh day. And in your Book we read this as a presage that when our work in this life is done, we too shall rest in you in the Sabbath of eternal life, though our works were very good only because you have given us the grace to perform them."[14] Less the summit than the sum of creation, the Sabbath is the sum of time: its summation or, better still, its summons.

Needful as the secularization of time may be for Augustine, it is not everything and would not pretend to be. It is only one aspect of the dialectic that links the two cities and that, for being binary, can all the more remarkably afford to shun the warmed-over dualism of the sacred and the profane. Articulating the interface of two cities desirous of each other, this dialectic is focused on hallowing time by secularizing it and timing the eternal.

Heidegger was not wrong: it is, he wrote in 1924, "the theologian who is the specialist of time, and indeed, if memory serves us correctly, theology has had to deal with time in many different ways."[15] This is so for the simplest of reasons—namely, that "the Christian faith falls into place in connection with time," and better still, "when the time is fulfilled." To be sure, one immediately thinks among other things of the incarnation. But does Heidegger himself really think of it, too? I wonder. Especially since he contends that because "theology treats human existence (*menschliches Dasein*) in its being before God," it treats "its temporal being in its relation to eternity." Very well. But at whose expense?

Must one drive a wedge between time and eternity and do so under the sheer pretense that the incarnation, if not the creation, consisted of withdrawing human existence from time? Or, in contrast with philosophy, must theology necessarily be viewed as bound to a God ineluctably taken for granted? This is nevertheless what Heidegger suggests or seems to do.

First, he says that, unlike the theologian, the philosopher himself will attempt to "understand time exclusively from the basis of time," even in terms of what he will call intratemporality. This intratemporality, writes Ricoeur, amounts to putting "the accent on the present, just as fundamental temporality puts it on the future and historicity puts it on the past."[16] Indeed, for Heidegger himself, intratemporality consists of putting the accent on the now of time in such a way that, transformed, the question

"What is time?" becomes the question "Who is time?"[17] This is the question that, from one echo to another, calling on us to witness, summons us to testify before the bar of time. Then by the time this question sinks in our hearing, it is heard as asking, "Who is the shepherd of time?" It is heard with an urgency so devoid of the least parody that one feels compelled to honor Heidegger's obsession with exactness, not to mention his preoccupation with authenticity, especially since, awake to that very question, he adds, "Am I my time?"

Sein und Zeit was to be published at least three years later, but Heidegger already puts the question and, assuming it is correctly put, infers that "then being-here would mean: to be is to be put in question."[18] Presumably had it not been for Heidegger's own circumspection about it, he could as well have defined the incarnation: the being through which God is here, a fortiori, is the being of that which is put in question.

"Who do you say that I am?" That is really the question, and not only Jesus puts it but also, in a like mood, anyone who in Christ has passed from death to life. It is the question that, in whatever way one understands this "I," both eludes and stays every reply, as does the Eternal One who forgets himself in time—or a father in his son. And though the metaphor hurts even the language of faith, "God becomes man" just as Peter heard himself told more or less abruptly.[19] The question still is without reply so long as, like Cain facing up to God, I want to escape from time instead of "redeeming" it; or I want to lock it in a clock instead of locking the clock into it; or again I want to shortchange its data by ransoming the future or by counterfeiting the past instead of investing them in that which precisely would time and vest them with a "present."

In contrast with the idea of time escheating itself into a downfall from which accordingly we need to rise up again to some timeless origin of a time before time, here we deal with the idea that time is being "accomplished," for the time being. Fulfilled time is time happening and coming to pass only if our liberation is not passed by and the world is transfigured. It happens or comes to pass when man and woman are time and again beckoned by that which, for being human, all too human, is the very condition without which God would not be God. And just this, in the mirror, not of nature or history but of creation and pleroma (fulfillment), in the mirror of the Christ as emblematic worlding of the word, of language, just this is what is at stake in the biblical dialectic of secularization and hallowing—of the worlding of the word.

Anachronistic Time and Eternal Now

God speaks and the thing happens: man or woman speaks and the word imparts them to one another, and neither is apart from the other. On the seventh day there is neither Greek nor Jew, neither male nor female. The times are fulfilled, and ushered in is a virtual image of the eschaton, of God's reign, of which, on the third day, the empty tomb is the proleptic emblem. "Christ is risen": he dis-covers death and, but for the divine if ironic ambiguity of language, points to death as that which, because it objectivates time—"the hour has come"[20]—forfeits its claim on life. Time is turned inside out. Easter, as Barth would say, comes before Good Friday. And for Bultmann, history is swallowed up by eschatology.[21] Or time, if it has a cutting edge, cuts a covenant with God, the eternal. Desacralizing nature and its dominion, a covenant with God is woven through time. Betokening God and man or woman with one another, this covenant releases them from the shackles of the sacred (as illustrated by such symbols as Egypt or the primordial tohu-bohu). At the same stroke, the covenant defatalizes history: there is no way of genealogically linking the clay fashioned by God and the breath through which "natural man" is toppled over into the human. Because history explains away whatever it seeks to explain, there is no way either of linking new and old covenants, Israel and the church. They are but occasions to whose timing one can only leap as though from nowhere—as does Abraham from Ur.

Abraham is therefore no mere ancestor but the father of all believers, Gentiles as well as Jews. Whatever continuity there is between Israel and the nations, it is a product neither of nature nor of history; it is created by God,[22] and to that extent it is secularized. It is also broken: it calls for a new covenant to be shared by Jews and Gentiles alike, as are the bread and wine among those that have broken with their respective past and are raised from the dead and gathered to the paschal fellowship of the New Being (as Tillich might say).

But this is a fellowship that is proleptic rather than anamnestic. It is a fellowship whose reality is eschatological. It is not the product of some saving history or some selective nature. And yet, *sub specie aeternitatis* (i.e., so far as eternity goes), in their fulfillment as proleptic emblems of the eternal, of the eschaton, time itself is fulfilled: it becomes timely—a *kairos*, as Tillich would say. Rather than some kind of principle overriding or overrunning time, this eschatic *kairos* is neither a beginning nor an end of time, much less a midpoint. It is the "milieu" of time, of that which precisely happens once and for all and constantly restructures time.

Time does not keep time. It is anachronistic. Whether cosmological or chronological, far from being eschewed, or reduced, or even denied any finality, *sub specie aeternitatis* it lies "in God's hand." That is, it has a destination, even a predestination, should this be understood in terms not of fate but of an eschatological "analysis"—a reconfiguration—through which the fatefulness of time is . . . "deconstructed."[23] Or else God would be God only outside of time. Rather, even for God, it takes time to be God. But God neither runs out of nor is exhausted by time. And the time it takes God to be God is eternal: it is eschatological time. It both encompasses and is the milieu of the time that, beginning and ending with the time given us once and for all, is for us a time of decision, a time when God, equally distant from or near to us all, is all in all.[24]

Anachronistic again, from creation to pleroma by way of incarnation, time that passes has no past. It has no past because it does not pass. And, J.-B. Pontalis points out, "time which does not pass is not the negation of time which passes. It is the fulfillment of it." As Jesus puts it: "Before Abraham was, I am."[25] Deconstructed as well as reconfigured are then "all our conceptions of time: of cyclical time, if we consider the rotation of our planet or the periodic return of the seasons; of evolutionary time, if we refer to the development of species and of the organism; of linear time, not following a straight line but a broken line, if we retrace the course of human history." Ironically put, it is as if time itself consisted, as would any kind of deconstructive analysis, in going against the grain of "our common perception: that of the years which slip through our fingers, that of the dizzy fall of grains of sand in the hour glass, that of our days and their own rhythm, that of our bodies and spirit when we feel them gain in strength or decline"[26]—for the time being.

What the skin is to the body the eschatic is to the temporal: the eschatic encompasses the temporal, even as the skin cloaks the body. Either way of putting it recalls the daring and yet cryptic bluntness of the psalmist's defiant faith when he utters, "My times are in your hand." So far so good. While more concrete because of its plural form, "times" also sounds more literal than (life)time would and illustrates a general claim of this essay—namely, that nothing is more symbolic than the literal. In fact, "times" says less than the former and more than the latter. The literal is more than merely literal. The symbolic is more than merely symbolic. Neither is more nor less of what the other is. Each of them oscillates between one extreme and the other. In the psalmist's utterance, time oscillates between the eternal and the ephemeral: it happens once and for all and confines both to the ultimate (eschatic) and to the proleptic (provisional and iterative). Never too literal to be symbolic, words are more telling than concepts. Words are kaleidoscopic, concepts unilateral.

Rather than half-full or half-empty, the bottle is both. The literal is by itself no more literal than the symbolic is by itself symbolic. That which happens once and for all is no less eternal for being ephemeral.

Eternity is to time as creation is to nature (or to history). The Big Bang would no longer be a big bang if we could go back to the time before it happened. Conversely, eternity is no protection against the ephemeral, against that which happens once and for all. Yet through all these terms, we belong not to an order of things but to an order of words. We belong to the realm of language. And yet we still want to make a name for ourselves; we want to be under the protection of a name, a rule, a foundation, and do not realize that, precisely, no protection is ever to come by if it should come with strings attached, with flag waving, with a safety net. No language can immunize us against any evil, much less against ourselves or against the enemy within ourselves. It can be bent enough to incur the pretense of a "final vocabulary," whatever its obedience, or to drag us into unwitting complicity with some "final solution," whatever its obsession. The question of divinity, as Charles Hartshorne contends, is so fundamental that even the basic rules of our language must either require or exclude God. But since God is a word woven together with other words of the human lexicon, we should not forget that even God, let alone the God of power, lies in the hands of a language bared to the utmost of its powerless power. Or, as Kierkegaard would say, we should not forget that through the Christ, God appears divested of all glory.[27]

Divested of glory, God is so contingent upon language as to lie in it and to be belied by it. Even the power of language has no power over what is brought forth through its ministrations. Unlike the sacred, language has no power of administration. It shepherds the worlding of the word—but only to the extent that its efficacy is as precarious as God is contingent upon it. A contingent God, rather than going by this or that name, is a God woven into words. They are words through which is in turn spun a world with no meaning of its own other than through other words. They are words that, because they address us to one another, are woven into a language that shepherds the solitary human being into the solidarity of being human and is no sooner spoken than we are spoken for. And we speak up, but with no net, with no one in the name of whom we could or should do so, just as the God that speaks is nameless and does not speak in the name of God.

God has no name but is a word among the words of a language through which the world breaks into words, knitting us together from birth to death, from faith to faith; spoken without a net, they are spoken once and for all. This is not unlike time, which does not "last" if only because per se, aside from not being everlasting, it neither refers us to some time before time nor defers us to some time after life. Time only happens; it happens like a gift—the unexpected gift of a reprieve, an "extension."[28] It does not lag, as it were, between birth and death, beginning and end, but is an occasion for their biological difference to be relieved—"redeemed," as Scriptures put it[29]—and transfigured into the once and for all experience of a lifetime. Time is no occasion for postponing life or returning to some primordial womb of all that is—for the time being—as though it were extruded from that which is eternal.

At one and the same stroke of the eschaton, time is both measured and without measure: either way, it times with that which is eternal. Likewise, we are told, God forms an alliance with day and night as God forms an alliance with man or woman,[30] and yet the days of such an alliance are numbered. Timing with the eternal, it spends once and for all the time when God, for being eternal, is a God with whom only "that comes which . . . is present" and yet is the wholly other.[31] Present or absent, and though word become flesh, God remains wholly other and yet is that of which the human is not lacking, for the literal is no lack of the symbolic. Nor is God what the world is lacking and compensates by brimming with idols that deceive its worldhood, its secularity, its timing with the word that becomes flesh and turns this world into a parable of the kingdom and utopia of God's love, here and now. In Christ, God is no more the measure of all that is than, for being human, the human being is the measure of God.

This is the case not only when the word becomes flesh, but also when it creates or when, all in all, it fulfills all that is—also when, so to speak, assuming time, God forgets that God is eternal: God is God only by reason of being contemporaneous with humans even as with the world. And it is a world so loved by God that, whether maximized as God's *shekinah* or minimized to the rootlessness of just a tent,³² it shelters, even for God, a passion for love and justice, here and now. It is a world so loved by God that, here and now, it is not so much God or, conversely, "man" who is the measure of all that is, but the Christ.

Take Adam. As figure of that by which God is known, Adam, far from being some first man, is neither more nor less than that human being for whom being human comes first. Or take Jesus, and God is viewed, not by comparison with what used to be referred to as "man par excellence," but in terms of that through which nothing *becomes* a human being save being human *tout court*, at last. Instead of beings and being-itself, with the former deferring to the latter as a minus to a plus sign, every being is all there is of that which happens and is once and for all. In the Christ-event, the flesh is for our sake all there is of that eternal word in whose light, if "to live is Christ," it is to live once and for all.

What in a bottle of water stands for the eternal is not the bottle but the water. Water is found in nature. The bottle adds nothing to water. Water alone is symbolic of life, of the eternal, of the worlding of the word, though *not without* language. And because words are to be found in nature no more than God is, in this or in that, God is likewise forever "wholly everywhere and nowhere contained wholly."³³ This is another way of saying that God can no more than time be objectified, although neither need be without an object, be it the eternal now.

In its classical version, this eternal now is more like a quiescent present that would not pass away,³⁴ yawning as it were between past and future and yet relieved from the frustrating contrast between "already" and "not yet," or suspended from the concreteness of time. The eternal now accounts for a mystique, not for an ethic, of time; it accounts for a both/and mystique rather than for an either/or ethic whose two prongs are related to one another as are the inside and outside of a Möbius strip. This strip lies neither inside nor outside but on their mutual edge, everywhere and nowhere symbolizing less a both/and process of continuity/discontinuity than an either/or iteration of a leap, a decision (Bultmann) one must take if, given one's past, one must jump onto the departing future, now.

Hegel comes to mind, and it dawns on him that "only the present is" and so concretely, moreover, that "the real present is thus eternity," although at this point Heidegger himself not surprisingly demurs. His time zone is obviously different from Hegel's, or so he would claim. His discord with Hegel and contrary appearances notwithstanding, the position he delineates actually comes rather close to chiming with the biblical approach to time. Though he seems critical of it, too, what in fact he denounces is a series of interpretations to which, under the guise of objectivity and historical correctness, it has so been coerced. It has been so coerced that time looks more like it must yawn between already and not yet than like a dehiscence of that which, being eternal, happens at all forever if it happens now, once and for all. "The being of time is the now," writes Heidegger, "but to the extent that every now is no longer 'now' or is not yet 'now,' it can be equally grasped as non-being."[35] But then it would seem that, for Heidegger, even when derived from the biblical tradition, a dialectic of "already/not yet" simply curbs the latter's eschatic dimension. It historicizes eschatology, reducing salvation to the history of salvation.

The biblical notion of timing (*kairos*) does not rest on some time differential that would have us caught between "already" and "not yet." It consists, instead, of a twofold proleptic deferral of the temporal to the eternal and, reciprocally, of the eschatic to that which, happening, can only happen once and for all, as intimated by typically topological and tropological expressions like "in spite of," "and yet" (*et tamen*).[36] In this connection, we must always remember that, signifiers being of themselves empty, the Ark of the Covenant is empty. It shelters what it is itself sheltered by—namely, the Law. It has no other "milieu" than Torah, the word of God, by which it is encompassed. This is not unlike the tomb, which is likewise empty, and yet in spite of that, "he is risen."

Entwining this eschatological approach to time with his notion of faith as eschatic existence, Paul develops an ethic whose dynamics oscillates back and forth between its anthropological, horizontal dimension and its theological, vertical dimension and defers God to the human being's quest for being human while conversely deferring the "being of time" to the worlding of that very word without which God would not be, would be no God, would be an idol.

At stake in this ethic of faith is a world whose actual configuration is polarized by the notion that, on the one hand, no human being would be in search of being human were it not for God or, even, for would-be gods; and that, on the other hand, no God is God, because in the world per se there can be no God, only idols. Equally at stake in this ethic is hence the worldhood of the world—a world whose idols, to which it reduces the divine,

Worlding the Word | 119

deprive it of its worldhood and cancel out the secular dimension to which it is entitled so far as it is a world for which God makes room, even as language makes room for the real. And the world, denied and emptied of its worldhood, is restored to it through the victory of faith—a victory over a world as emblematically empty as, in the horizontal dimension, is the tomb on the third day, and death is then only the way of all flesh. But in the vertical dimension, death itself is not all there is to time. A symbol of our utmost contingency, death is and remains a symbol, though again not *merely* a symbol. Dying and the consciousness of it, unlike death, points beyond itself—and not to some mythical otherworldly life after death. In spite of death, dying points to that ultimately ethical and most world-affirming fiction of a faith that, as eschatic existence, is beckoned by just that which, for not being eternal, is unprecedented—namely, time.

Paul's ethic of faith is no otherworldy ethic but an ethic of time. It focuses on that which, for not having been programmed, seems all the more relevant and is all the more urgent for seeming unrealizable, beyond reach of all that is possible. It is an ethic of the impossible as the only alternative to every solution possible. It is an ethic of the new—a new being, a new heaven, and a new earth—an ethic of a new world unfettered by ideological illusions that straitjacket the utopian streak of its worldhood.

Timing the world, the word is worlded; and the world comes into its own whenever God speaks and the thing happens, and the tomb is empty, and, to begin with, "the earth [is] without form and void." The God who creates is a God that makes a new thing. And nothing is new unless, with creation as with time, there is nothing that comes before the new. Of a different order from that of nature or of history, the new is proleptic. We do not become used to it until, embodied by the desire for yet another new thing, it does not repeat itself as customs do but calls for new norms and again a new thing.

A case is today made in this regard by the claim of a discrepancy between ethics and morals, between the ethical and the moral. Whether this contention is arbitrarily construed or not, the issue it has triggered has no doubt the benefit of a widespread fascination and points to the fact that no decision-making process can today rely on experience alone (as morality tends to claim and ethics claims to the contrary). Accountable for our past, we are, moreover, no less accountable for unpredictable effects above and beyond predictable ones, given the industrialization and mechanization of life itself. We have to think of a future, always a surprise but increasingly a future of which we have no experience. The lesson our morality has drawn from the past does not help us to cope with a future, the expectation of which is as likely as not to upset the apple cart of our moral memory. In lieu of a retrospective morality we are impelled, compelled, to devise a prospective ethic that, we hope, will cope with the aftermath of what we might globally call a technological revolution in every one of our projects, material or existential. To that extent, distinguishing moral and ethical might make sense.

The fact is that a new quest for ethical norms or values is in the offing. To say the least, it is bent on displacing, on disqualifying, age-old compacts between morality and an increasingly hypothetical natural law. Still, alleging a discrepancy between "moral" and "ethical" may be only a fad, at best a matter of linguistic idiosyncrasy. It is no less instructive. Longevity was of old an excuse for wisdom. It is now subject at worst to obsolescence and at best to novelty. Accumulated experience does not automatically account for its renewal in the face of unprecedented action. An ethic of time is an ethic for which there is a time for everything, and everything is for a time. A "provisional" ethic, it has lost the taste of what it calls and yearns for—namely, a utopia, be it a Promised Land or the kingdom of God, if one should want illustrations from the Bible.

Canaan, the land of milk and honey, was a surprise to the children of Israel. Spiritually, culturally, socially, and politically, the disciples of Jesus surely had no idea of the extent to which, in keeping with the worlding of the word, the notion of the body of Christ as emblem of God's kingdom and its principle of equity among all would in later centuries reverberate throughout the body social and politic.

Far from implying a relativistic ethic or from relativizing morality, time retrieves and cancels as it cancels and retrieves the old—and heralds the new. And because it allows or suffers both iteration and innovation, dos and don'ts as well as either/or, time at one and the same time encompasses both delegation and obligation, both derogation and rogation. All the more urgent for being relative to its time, to that which happens once and for all, every ethical demand relays an eschatological imperative whose urgency compels it to keep from running out of time. Not only does it accordingly radicalize time, it also secularizes time. And secularized time is time redeemed.

As timing of the eternal and its glory, redeemed time is no secondhand eternity. No more than the creation, which rather than happening within does not happen without time, the incarnation happens not so much within as *not without* time. It hosts the eternal yet *not without* radicalizing it through the secular even as the spirit is through the flesh. An ethic of time is an ethic of incarnation. Geared on the two dialectic prongs of word and flesh, of the holy and the secular, it is concerned with so worlding the word that the worldhood of the world in turn chimes with timing the eternal. And it is so concerned with worlding the word that, in spite of though not without the world, it embodies an "opportunity for the good," which, as Calvin writes in his Commentary on Colossians (4:5), we can only and must "seize."[37] It embodies a *kairos,* which under Paul's pen seems to have demoted itself, dulled into *chronos,* and despite Tillich's lofty conceptual arrangement of it must yet be redeemed.

Indeed, words are not concepts. And concepts can even muzzle words. Concepts are not porous. And unlike concepts, but like time and eternity or ethical and moral, words are porous. What the Bible means by time takes so many different words that, as James Barr has shown, it is practically impossible to extract a unified concept.[38] As a matter of fact, this could even mean that, for the Bible, time simply "is-not-everything," as Lacan would say. Eternity likewise. No more than a mathematician's whole of wholes is a concept of the "all"—or of any kind of totality—to be found in the Bible. Similarly but on another level, man and woman cannot become one unless they remain two (Lacan). Nor am I who I am except in relation to another. Relation, a matter of time, postulates otherness, especially if, growing into mutual respect as well as self-respect, it grows into that solidarity which transcends selective or restrictive pseudo-solidarities of identity and difference proper only to tribalism, whether cultural or religious, racial or sexual. Solidarity always lies beyond itself. It is not a matter of identity or of difference but of otherness.

Faced with the identical or the different, the self is always threatened, if not from without, at least surely from within. The danger to oneself always lies within the self. It lies with the self that, faced with the other, feels sufficiently alike to feel threatened or sufficiently different to feel indifferent. Otherness is neither difference nor indifference. It is a desire for that which one is not lacking—and is not ever lacking unless one's time is up.

Mortal by nature, we are not meant to live on expectations of a substitute for death, of some style of metempsychosis or another. Once and for all we can only hold ourselves accountable for the time imparted to us and redeem it, should we be ourselves redeemed. This mortal nature of ours we must honor by living up to it without defrauding it. Death—and, through death, time—is not so much what crowns as what in the end neutralizes nature, which knows no evil. Conversely, time is, in spite of death, that through which God is radically enfranchised from nature, which knows no evil. Only God hates evil. Only God confronts us with a choice between life and death. And only God can go so far as to love Jacob and hate Esau, who trades his birthright for a lentil soup and, instead of living up to this right he thinks he deserves, plays for time and wastes it.

God hates to waste time. And time wasted is time not timing with itself—or, for that matter, with God. We must, in this connection, revisit the notion of predestination. Particularly giving Calvin his due, we must realize that the "pre" of predestination signifies not that our destiny has been determined before any merit on our part but that it can only be, and is assumed in spite of, what we deserve or do not deserve. It serves to stress that but for the grace of God, we would all be condemned to death. Nature being what it is, Calvin does not say that we are mortal because we are sinful. Rather, he says that being mortal, we can only be sinful before God and that we should have no choice other than death. But because we are sinful only before God, there must be and there is an alternative.[39] There is another way of dying. Paul hints at this when he writes that "death is the wages of sin."[40] There is also another way of living, and Calvin tackles this issue with his notion of predestination.

What I mean with this notion of predestination is that what Calvin is tackling is the problem of time from the standpoint of the incarnation, its "intemporation" (some would say) or its way of worlding the word. Aside from the existential, anthropological dimension of the incarnation, the worlding of the word has also a cosmological dimension, especially if the Christ, being the "secret" of the former, must also be the pivot of the latter. Predestination is thus Calvin's way of viewing time in the mirror of the word become flesh. Time no more than predestination has an *"archē,"* a meaning-giving principle that lies in nature or history. It is as anarchic as the worlding of the word. Enraged neither by history (fate) nor by any kind of natural determinism, it is goaded by the crook of that shepherd of time that is the eternal word.

Speaking of time, the Bible not only feels no need to stick with a single word but also seems rather unperturbed by its apparent lack of a definite word for eternity. Nothing, not even the weather, is for the Bible more changing than time—except perhaps the word itself. And nothing, the seasons included, reflects time and its moods better than language, whose primacy governs the biblical tradition. That is why, iconoclastic and prophetic, the hermeneutic method it develops rests on the assumption that, not unlike utensils, the meaning of words depends on their use. It is not the shape or the form of a utensil but its use that determines a kettle.[41] A word is likewise that which goes on acquiring meaning. From one phrase to another, it does not necessarily have the meaning it had at first. In some way a word already consists not so much in maintaining as in translating its meaning—from one language to another, as it were. This is so much the case that the Hebrew *'olam* is rendered in Greek by *aion,* which in turn becomes *saeculum* in Latin, while *pleroma* indifferently refers to *chronos* as well as to *kairos.* And *kairos* itself, used alike to indicate both an opportunity and a season,[42] serves finally to focus the fulfillment of time on the worlding of the word, on "the grace which has been given us in Jesus Christ before eternity,"[43] that is, in view of what in Greek is called time lasting through the times (*pro chronon aionion*) and in Latin is rendered by *ante tempora saecularia* (times ago)!

The paradox of time: it is infinite so long as it has not come to an end, so long as it is in the hands of God, of the eternal word—even of the One under whom Isaiah stands and tries to understand through that most audacious language, that of the prophet who upsets every preconceived idea regardless of some sacred chain of being it sanctions or the particular logic of time it charters. Unfazed, he declares, "You are my witnesses, says the Eternal. . . . Before me, no god was formed, and after me there will be none. . . . You are my witnesses, says the Eternal, and I am God."[44] No God is God without us, and still less is the eternal a shepherd. This amounts to saying that a person—even Jewish—is a person who knows that she or he is not God. But then is it enough for a person to know it?

Indeed, if Jesus is the Christ through whom God is not God without us, or if God is a God who "becomes man," or, better still, if God is a God through whose being we are being human or through whose word we are spoken for, then what this means is that, unlike the Jew who knows that no human being is per se being human or that no human is God, Jesus is a Jew who does not take himself for God. He knows not only that he is mortal but also that he must die. He dies—at one with himself if not with God, and alone. And even God is spared death: God is no dying and rising God. Jesus simply "temporalizes" God, just as the incarnation, secularizing what happens once and for all, secularizes time, enfranchising God no less from the history of the nations (Luke) than from that of Israel (Matthew), much as Israel itself once was freed from the shackling gods of nature.

In Christ, God happens; God comes to pass through the human, and once and for all, time passing is no past time. Or, to repeat, God is not an ancestor but a father, indeed an adoptive father. "You are my witnesses, you whom I have chosen,"[45] says God, the Eternal One in whom "we have life, movement and being,"[46] in whom we have time until, reminding us as well as Job of what is at stake, God throws in our face the question, "The rain, has it a father?"[47] Wretched father, who would be father only according to nature! Or who would be father but only in order to prove that the natural order was off-limits to the eternal! But God is to be neither assimilated with nature nor estranged from it. And biblical time is neither cyclic nor linear. It is not that biblical time ignores the seasons or "the year, the day, the hour: these are concepts which are inseparable from the biblical witness to the divine revelation."[48] So they are, however, only in the light of the Sabbath.

Ecce Homo

The biblical approach to time is sabbatical. It calls for the hallowing of time. Liturgical would, therefore, be just as appropriate a description of it. And because the hallowing of time and the secularization of the eternal now ultimately hinge on one another, this approach is ruled not by an anamnestic process but by the proleptic dialectic of sin and grace—in other words, by the incarnation, by the worlding of the word. This is a dialectic of which the two horns can also be described as nature (desacralized) and history (defatalized) or as creation and pleroma (fulfillment). Or again it is a dialectic of the ultimate and the new (*eschaton* and *novum*), hence is eminently liturgical, though not necessarily in the mystical so much as in the ethical, social, political sense of public action the term originally referred to. As interface of the eternal and the temporal, of heaven and earth, of church and world, the liturgy thus aims less to "represent" the eternal than to secularize it (preaching) insofar as, conversely, it aims at the sanctification of time (sacrament).[49] Essentially proleptic, the liturgy is a prophetic act. But since this act involves the so-called priesthood of all believers, the liturgy must of necessity entwine the religious and the secular. In this sense, the liturgy can also be viewed as a charismatic act. It consists in redeeming the time when the opportunity presents itself—or when the word becomes flesh.

Barth himself did not fail to stress this: "The word has become flesh" means also "the word has become time"[50] and the time is fulfilled—as happens at Easter. Or even as already happens when God blesses the seventh day and hallows it and "thus the world is being worlded all the while it is created [through the word]"[51]—and, from beginning to end, God makes all things new.[52]

Still, is there anything which, like the new, reminds us more of the old, indeed of the past, even while timing us with the future? On the seventh day, the Sabbath does just that. Symbolic of the kingdom of God, it stands for the otherness of time and ushers in the end of time, its fullness. But this fullness of time or its eschatic otherness, what is it if not, time and again, an opportunity for its ultimate rehearsal, its *kairos*—world without end? Enduring time, such is the Sabbath, which breaks with nature and even breaks with time that passes as it breaks with the ritual of the previous six days and yet is their fulfillment. Just because it then fulfills no less than God's own work, it also breaks with the ritual of work: work does not exhaust God any more than time exhausts eternity.

Or, to quote Ecclesiastes, time is only when, world without end, there is a time for everything,[53] that is, when the word is being worlded. "As long as the earth endures, seedtime and harvest, cold and heat, summer and winter, day and night, will never cease."[54] In the eschatic perspective of the Sabbath, time is infinite as long as it is not ended—fulfilled. But then it is neither finite nor infinite. Towed, as it were, by the Sabbath in its eschatic thrust, time is the denegation of the self-negation that would befall time if it were without beginning and end. And were it hypothetically eternal, eternity would only be the negation, not the denegation, of time. Temporal is thus, by contrast, that denegation which occurs *on* time as well as *in* time—world without end. And fulfilled at last is man or woman—*ecce homo*—whose days are numbered and who, rather than dying of it, lives up to it and lives it up, once and for all.

This phrase, "once and for all," has at least the peculiarity of equally fitting the temporal and the eternal, the ephemeral and the everlasting. It also fits the dialectic of being and speaking, of wording and worlding, even of the religious and the secular—all those twin poles of language. Variants of these can be named as the universal and the singular, or in a more trivial fashion, what we seem bound to stumble on when an old paradigm abruptly shifts into a new one and we are caught within a destiny without destination, a goal with no way to reach it, given where we come from.

Epilogue

The Two Hands of Language: A Secular Christ

Where do we go from here? The question is obviously rhetorical at least so far as the next stage has been adumbrated all along and so far as we know where we come from.

The issue? Call it secularization, a short-cut term whose connotations have mostly been negative.[1] But the process of which this term is characteristic is no more a secret to the biblical tradition of hallowing than creation or the incarnation is to its understanding of faith as eschatic existence. In other words, "worlding the word" is what biblically lies at the root of what we, even derogatorily, call secularization: God speaks and the thing happens. Whether in terms of transcendence or immanence, this process not only copes with acculturating or worlding the word but also is concerned with the worldhood of the world and with both its religious and its secular dimension. The process may waver, and historically has, but in keeping with biblical faith the concern has in the main been consistently upheld. This is not a surprise, either, given Israel's fundamental option for history over nature.

But history is not enough. The story of Israel also rings like an unending confession of sins. From the prophets to Jesus, history turns into a story the balance of which they all warn against, in fact urging their listeners to assume it and "make it history!" by breaking off with it. Otherwise, one is confronted with the worst kind of secularization possible, which lies in sacralizing a tradition and is a temptation to which even Israel is not immune.[2] This is a temptation that the Hebrew Bible, somewhat straining its own genius, spells out in a caution: Should you ever meet God, you are dead.[3] This is a rather harsh warning against anyone who would reduce the holy to the secular, or unspeakable transcendence to sheer babbling immanence. By and large, the holy lies in hallowing the name as well as the world. The intrinsic goodness of creation is never lost sight of. Nor is it subsequently forgotten by the Christian tradition, contrary temptations notwithstanding. The emergence of a so-called secular world cannot then be explained in terms only of the gradual demise of Christianity, of which it may also be the legitimate product, especially if the current situation is viewed in a global perspective rather than from a merely Western standpoint.

Is the secular not equally the secret of Eastern religions? At the opposite end of the spectrum from Western fascination with a world beyond this world, think of the rather sly counsel given the Eastern seeker of wisdom, no spark of which could ever take him or her out of this world, a world so real as never to seem real enough. The counsel? Bluntly expressed, it says: "Should you ever meet the Buddha, kill him." The East is as brashly receptive to the secular as the West pretends to be preciously suspicious of it, courting it all the while. In an increasingly globalizing world, East and West are impelled into reflecting (on) one another, not so much because of specific religious traditions or gods, as because of the one thing they have in common, which also stands in need of being worded if the world that must be born of it is to be one of compassion and solidarity between human beings on their respective way of being human. That thing they have in common is the secular—by reason of which the gospel says, "You cannot see God unless you see Jesus, unless you see to it that, even through Jesus, a human being lies in merely being human."[4]

Language equally debunks the divine and the human, transcendence and immanence, the religious and the secular, or, under the pretext of identity and community, the obsession with parochialism, whether Eastern or Western. "In Christ," Paul contends, "there is neither Jew nor Greek." And yet Paul remains a Jew. He never pretends to be the last of the Jews: the cross to which Jesus is nailed is, and remains, for him a stumbling block. But then just that is the reason why he can rebuke his fellow Jews, each of whom would rather be the last Jew—if not a Jew first amidst all those goyim. It is why, too, at the other end of the spectrum—Athens—he subtly rebukes his listeners. Hearing Paul's message as a demonstration of folly, the Athenians cannot help but, individually and collectively, amidst barbarians, think of themselves as Greek first.

Marcion comes to mind.[5] Dubbed arch heretic of all times, even before Christian thought has dawned on the West, Marcion tackles the same issue. Obsessed with the incarnation of the word, he does survey the Old

Testament but only in view of making it history, turning faith in Christ into the seal of an orphan religion, a religion as suspicious of the past as it is of the world of Greeks and Jews to which it is born. The incarnation falls short of its mark—namely, the worlding of the word or iconoclastic dimension of a faith in the light of which commitment to God and involvement in the world are equally constitutive of both its reality and its truth. As would Marcion, Paul does say that we no longer know the Christ according to the flesh. But his way of deconstructing this language is no less iconoclastic of the cultural (or, for that matter, the secular) and its Greek acme than it is of the religious and its Jewish epitome. No sooner has Saul stopped viewing the Christ according to the canons of his religious forebears than Paul depicts a Christ through whose design as interface of the divine and the human he is drawing a figure of speech, which is all the more christophoric for being attuned to a nascent secular situation and for aiming at the transcendence of otherwise irreconcilable presuppositions. Though we must think "globally," we can only believe "locally," beholden as we are to our various dialects and still short of a *koinē,* of a secular Christ. Inasmuch as for Paul what Jews and Greeks, or East and West, have in common is, rather than God, a world full of gods[6]—namely, the secular.

Yes, the Greek gods dance, the Buddha smiles, and the biblical god speaks. But what are speaking, or smiling, or dancing, or dogma and poetry if not forms of a language equally distant from the divine and the human, the natural and the spiritual, the literal and the symbolic, the religious and the secular? Depending on cultural circumstances, the accent may fall on one or the other within each of these pairs. But within none of them can one element be shorn of the other without being drastically, even fatally, impaired. True, the secular was already disenchanted with dogma when it was bruised by the growing—brutal and yet redeemable—impact of techno-scientific knowledge upon our age-old or (not to resist a hallowed word) secular wisdom. Weaned on milk of a mother tongue, we go on nursing, if not on being nursed, in the idiom in which this wisdom has reached and nurtured us. Idioms are markers of hospitality—of hostility, too, when its etymological twin, hospitality, is restrictive. Dogma is no exception to this kind of consideration. To paraphrase Lichtenberg, dogma can also amount to a mere personification of the inconceivable,[7] even as in the past God went, for example, by the name of this or that mountain.

There is no need to delve here into subtleties whether of semantics or semiotics and similar kinds of scientific inquiry about language. Pure and simple grammar is enough to point out that with "concept (of) God" we naturally think of God as a concept. And yet, with the "word (of) God" we do not usually think of God as word, much less as a word. In common usage, the word (of) God itself, somewhat hypostasized, is already on its way to personification, even though nothing is as allergic to idols as language. God hardly even occurs in some books of the Bible, for which God is language, precisely because God is a word.

Extremes meet: even the concept of God banks on this and is therefore worth a critique, even a rebuttal, but no contempt. The concept tries to drive language to its outermost orbit, whence it faces a reentry hazard should it in the process have become alienated from its initial linguistic atmosphere and thus belong to a symbol system no longer valid. This system is no longer valid, that is, except today by reason of some dubious poetic license among diehards of old patterns of belief, as Tillich points out in reviewing the classic proofs of the existence of God. Call it metaphysics or ontology, the demise of either or both of these extremes entails no dismissal of language as shepherd, though not as shepherd of some sacralized being but as shepherd of a human being into being human. Language lies in shepherding a biomechanistic animal into a speaking animal, whose being hangs on being worded, on transforming whatever power of being it harbors into a power of wording; in other words, on transforming a power whose use wears out into another whose use bears out.

Biologically, the power of being lurks in every human being that comes into the world prematurely and is immature. The lilies of the field or the birds of the air exemplify this power. The former neither work nor spin; the latter neither sow nor reap.[8] Like a bird that grows wings in exercising this power, the snail grows a shell. The human being does neither. Instead of growing a shell, he or she builds a house. Instead of growing wings, the human being builds the Concorde. The human being moves from the power of being to the power of wording and thereby becomes as vulnerably unique as he or she is irreplaceable, as singular as he or she is universal—a figure of Christ,[9] a figure as secular as it is (religiously speaking) Western. But this figure is neither so religious nor so secular that it cannot adopt or adapt to, or be spoken and heard through, "my" own mother tongue, a tongue on which I am bound to be weaned even as the symbolic is weaned on the literal. From a mere parrot of words (be they of Jesus), "I" become a speaking animal and, even as Jesus is enfranchised by the Christ, "I" become a christophoric human being—unlike the parrot, which, after all, can only speak its mother tongue.[10]

How much of a tongue, of an idiom, is a mother tongue and, correspondingly, how much of a language is it already? And to what extent can languages partake of each other as they must unless they naturally are stretched beyond their respective idiomatic molding?

Herald of the secularization of our Western idiom, even Nietzsche (or Derrida and Gadamer, if possibly not Heidegger) traces this secularization back to its initial molding in the hands of the word become flesh, in the hands of that language of which, with the exception of the Christ, we have all been but parrots at best. This is another way of saying, with no false modesty, that our Western idiom has developed under a specific imprint that it still behooves us to call christological. We call it this in spite of its past dogmatic resonance and, rather, in keeping with its primary referent, the primacy of word over being, of the worlding of the word become flesh, of the commingling of the religious and the secular as well as of the divine and the human. With both its hands, the religious and the secular, christology is a parabolic ellipse focused, on the one hand, on the autonomy of language (or anthropology) and, on the other, on its theonomous aspect insofar as we no sooner speak than we are spoken for. To that extent there is, as part of the Western contribution to a mutual understanding of religious idioms across a globalizing world, no better chance than a so-called secular Christ, one whose death on a cross makes no sense per se and is no more a natural phenomenon than is the resurrection. Even the risen Christ is a fiction of language if only because nothing is more symbolic than the literal, or more religious than the secular—much like an infamous cross that rises and raises a symbol from reprobation to forgiveness and reconciliation.

Where, then, do we go from here? Sketching as it were a triptych, so-called markers have gradually loomed on the horizon of a christomorphic understanding of language with its two hands rehearsing life and death,[11] the human and the divine, as well as salvation and the kingdom or self and the world, not to mention the universal and the singular, or the religious and the secular.

Geared on a reconfiguration of the word become flesh, the central panel of this triptych points to a christomorphic understanding of language. It points to the Christ as an event of language—never so symbolic an event as when, through its fiction, even a most naïve literal description of it is honored; never so religious either that its fulfillment is ever shy of the secular. In the light of this christomorphic triptych of language, one of the side panels picks up the biblical theme of God as word. Rather than being focused on God as (power of) being, it is focused on God as (power of) wording, even on wording God, though through no "words [but] of the tribe" (Mallarmé). Keyed likewise to the kingdom rather than to some world after death, the other panel illustrates neither more nor less than the worlding of the word, though there is no world but this secular one in which, living by faith, we may and do live once and for all.

As with John's unexcelled prologue, christomorphic language certainly consists in shepherding the real into a world come of age, a world come true, though never so literally as to fall irremediably short of a symbol, even of that least of all, the "purely" symbolic. Jesus comes to bear witness to truth in the world. But the way John puts it, what that witness is all about sounds as though it consists of a mutual shepherding of truth and the real, of the religious and the secular.[12] John's understanding of the incarnation is dyed as much in the temporal as it is in the eternal.[13] The difference being one of quality, not of quantity, no chasm yawns—so to speak—between the eternal and the temporal. John does not recoil from downscaling some supernatural Christ. He compels us to an about-face by getting us used to viewing things in the uncanny light of "a secular Christ." That is to say, we have not grasped John's notion of the word become flesh, even of God as wording, until or unless we realize it must so expand as to demand the worlding of that very word, extending it into secular relevance. Even Jesus calls for transvaluing, if not outright secularizing, the religious heritage to which he belongs—ironically, even to the point of dying of it on a cross.[14]

Notes

INTRODUCTION

1. This subject of the idol and its ambivalence has been noted by Jacques Maritain in "Signe et symbole," *Revue thomiste* 44 (April 1938): 315, and more recently by Jean-Luc Marion in *L'idole et la distance* (Paris: Grasset, 1977). Ever since *The Death of God: The Culture of Our Post-Christian Era* (New York: George Braziller, 1961 [© 1957]), I have myself coped with this topic against the background of a general contention regarding the iconoclastic dimension of biblical faith and have insistently kept from bartering iconoclasm (supposedly a misnomer) for "idoloclasm" (the smashing of idols), unable to warm up to the idea that no ultimate icon could ever become an idol. See my *Wait without Idols* (New York: George Braziller, 1964); *No Other God* (New York: George Braziller, 1966); *La condition de Dieu* (Paris: Éditions du Seuil, 1970).

1. THEOLOGY AND THE SECULAR

1. See Gabriel Vahanian, *Tillich and the New Religious Paradigm* (Aurora, Colo.: The Davies Group, 2004).

2. Clayton Crockett, foreword to Charles E. Winquist, *Epiphanies of Darkness* (Aurora, Colo.: The Davies Group, 1998).

3. See Vahanian, *No Other God*, where, incidentally, *mundum* should read *mundus*.

4. Cf. Saint Augustine, *Enchiridion* 30: "Man's good will precedes many of God's gifts, but not all; and among those which it does not precede it must be itself counted."

5. Martin Buber, *Eclipse of God: Studies in the Relation between Religion and Philosophy* (New York: Harper, 1957), 28; *The Writings of Martin Buber*, ed. Will Herberg (New York: Meridian Books, 1956); *To Hallow This Life: An Anthology*, ed. Jacob Trapp (New York: Harper and Brothers, 1958); Vahanian, *The Death of God*, 65.

6. Ernst Troeltsch, *The Social Teachings of the Christian Churches*, trans. Olive Wyon (London: George Allen & Unwin, 1951), 2:522.

7. Stanislas Breton, *L'avenir du christianisme* (Paris: Desclée de Brouwer, 1999), 133–34, 142.

8. Matthew 25; Galatians 3:28; Colossians 3:11. On the eschatological dimension of secularization, see Walter Jaeschke, "Saekularisierung," in *Handbuch der Religionswissenschaft* (Stuttgart: Kohlhammer, 2000).

9. Troeltsch, *The Social Teachings of the Christian Churches*, 49.

10. Hebrews 13:14; Philippians 3:20.

11. In his commentary on the Gospel of John (3:3), Calvin writes: "abused are those for whom heaven is the kingdom of God."

12. Matthew 25:40, 25:45.

13. Matthew 22:21; Mark 12:17; Luke 20:25; Psalm 137:4.

14. Greek Acts of Andrew 38:4–5.

15. Catherine Pickstock, *After Writing: On the Liturgical Consummation of Philosophy* (Oxford: Blackwell, 1998), 217; see also 189.

16. See Albert Camus, *The Fall* (New York: Alfred A. Knopf, 1957).

17. Commenting on the Gospel of John, Saint Augustine writes: "Understanding is the reward of faith." "We believe that we might know; for if we wished first to know and then believe, we should not be able either to know or to believe." In *Joannis evangelium tractatus* 29.6, 27.9, quoted from *An Augustine Synthesis*, arranged by Erich Przywara (New York: Harper Torchbooks, 1958), 58.

18. Saint Augustine, *Confessions*, trans. H. R. S. Pine-Coffin (Baltimore: Penguin Books, 1961), 11.26–27.

19. Saint Augustine, *The City of God* 12.3.

20. Saint Augustine, *The City of God* 15.7, as in C. N. Cochrane's rendering of it in *Christianity and Classical Culture* (Oxford: Oxford University Press, 1944), 500.

21. Saint Augustine, *The City of God* 11.1.

22. See Takashi Kato, "Le christianisme et les religions de l'Europe," in *L'Europe à la croisée des religions: L'enjeu théologique*, ed. Gabriel Vahanian (Strasbourg: Travaux de la Faculté de théologie, 1995).

23. Galatians 3:28; Colossians 3:11.

24. John 8:32.

25. See Richard Rorty, *Philosophy and the Mirror of Nature* (Princeton: Princeton University Press, 1979), 359.

26. To my knowledge this conjunction of anarchy and theocracy is nowhere explicitly made by Paul Tillich in *Écrits contre les nazis* (Paris: Cerf, 1994), 150, 232; and xcix, lxxiv of the introduction, by Jean Richard. It has utopic connotations and to that extent is suggested by depictions of the spirit of utopia whose claim to autonomy he bases on the "idea of natural harmony." Practically, he substitutes *kairos* for utopia. On anarchy and autonomy or objectification and social "ritualization" (i.e., on anarchy and ultimacy or "theocracy"), see Georg Simmel, *Secret et sociétés secrètes* (n.p.: Circé/poche, 1996), 85; also, more specially, Cornélius Castoriadis, for whom autonomy consists in putting oneself into question: "De

l'autonomie en politique: L'individu privatisé," *Le Monde diplomatique* 45 (February 1998): 23. On this view, objectivation differs from objectification in that the individual and the social are each other's objectivation so long as, in the name of life together, between them is maintained a certain degree of polarity and tension, the process of which is what I call objectivation. By contrast, both Rousseau's view of the social as a threat to the individual and the totalitarian view of the individual as a threat to the social vocation of humankind correspond to a unilateral objectification of this process and its denial. Science notwithstanding, even the world is an event, not a mere fact. And nothing is more heteronomous than the anarchist's claim that he needs no one to be governed by, not even a God; or the theocrat's claim that no human being deserves to be governed by another, but only by God. Anarchy and theocracy are each other's objectified twin. Though the word always needs to be worlded, they have deserted the domain of ideas for that of frozen ideologies, of faith for that of rituals, of language for that of things.

27. Genesis 4:9.

28. See 1 Corinthians 8; Charles E. Winquist, "The Silence of the Real," in *Theology at the End of the Century: A Dialogue on the Postmodern with Thomas J. J. Altizer, Mark C. Taylor, Charles E. Winquist, Robert P. Scharlemann,* ed. Robert P. Scharlemann (Charlottesville: University Press of Virginia, 1990); Zygmunt Bauman, *Postmodern Ethics* (Oxford: Blackwell, 1993), 30, 125, 181.

29. A practical implication of honoring the secular can be expressed by asking how it is possible to live in a planetary village beckoned by pluralism where we buy bread from the same baker as the adept of many another religion and celebrate communion, the Lord's Supper, or the Eucharist against the background of theories like transubstantiation, consubstantiation, or whatever other sacrificial symbol system.

30. Edith Wyschogrod, *Saints and Postmodernism: Revisioning Moral Philosophy* (Chicago: University of Chicago Press, 1990), xiii. With all due respect for an author's definition of specific terms, I cannot help but think that, in Wyschogrod's usage, "narratives," because they may be fictitious, sounds appropriate only by reason of a conscious overextension of the term in its normal significance. One is reminded of Edmond Jabès's innumerable quotations from an endless list of rabbis that never existed. They provide him with a scenario for his own writing. In like manner, life narratives seem to deal less with real stories than with possible scenarios for ethical commitment.

31. Zephania 1:5; 1 Corinthians 8:5; Matthew 8:21.

32. See Wyschogrod, *Saints and Postmodernism,* 14.

33. Jaroslav Pelikan, *Jesus through the Centuries: His Place in the History of Culture* (New Haven: Yale University Press, 1985), 141.

34. Ibid.

35. Jacques Le Goff, *La civilisation de l'Occident médiéval* (Paris: Arthaud, 1964), 253–54.

36. Ernst Cassirer, *The Philosophy of the Enlightenment* (Boston: Beacon Press, 1955), 138–39.

37. 2 Corinthians 8:15; Exodus 16:18.

38. Romans 4:8.

39. "The Freedom of a Christian" as well as "Secular Authority" are included in *Martin Luther: Selections from His Writings*, ed. John Dillenberger (Garden City, N.Y.: Anchor Books, 1961). On this question of salvation or the history of salvation, see in particular Rudolf Bultmann, *Theology of the New Testament*, trans. Kendrik Grobel, vol. 2 (New York: Charles Scribner's Sons, 1955), 8–9; Bultmann, "The Idea of God and Modern Man," in *Translating Theology into the Modern Age*, ed. Robert W. Funk and Gerhard Ebeling (New York: Harper and Row, 1965); Paul Tillich, *Theology of Culture* (Oxford: Oxford University Press, 1959), 44; Tillich, "Salvation," *Princeton Seminary Bulletin* 57 (1963): 1; Tillich, *Gesammelte Werke*, vol. 5 (Frankfurt am Main: Evangelisches Verlagswerk, 1980), 22–23; J. Christiaan Beker, "Biblical Theology Today," *Princeton Seminary Bulletin* 62 (1968); Gabriel Vahanian, ed., *Le salut: Du salut dans l'au-delà au salut sans au-delà* (Strasbourg: Publications de la Faculté de théologie protestante, 1994).

40. Michael Walzer, *The Revolution of the Saints: A Study in the Origins of Radical Politics* (London: Weidenfeld and Nicolson, 1966), 51.

41. Quoted from William G. McLaughlin, "The Diverse Origins of the American Tradition of Separation of Church and State," *Cimarron Review* 2 (1967): 50.

42. 1 Corinthians 8:4–6.

2. No God Is God

1. Marco Maria Olivetti, ed., *Incarnation*, Archivio di filosophia (Padua: Cedam, 1999), 13.

2. Karl Barth, *Die kirchliche Dogmatik* (Zollikon-Zürich: Evangelischer Verlag, 1944–45), vol. 1, part 1, §8.2, p. 341; Henri Bouillard, *Karl Barth* (Paris: Aubier, 1957), 1:232.

3. See Odes of Solomon 10:1–2.

4. 1 Corinthians 6:19, 3:16.

5. Pierre Bonnard, *L'épître de saint Paul aux Philippiens* (Neuchâtel: Delachaux et Niestlé, 1950), 61.

6. For Augustine, I am reminded by Maurice Boutin, the present has no space (*Confessions* 11; 27.34).

7. Leviticus 19:17.

8. Genesis 22:7.

9. Matthew 27:46.

10. Leviticus 19:17. Also worth mentioning in connection with a sacrifice of atonement, though they may not appreciate it, are René Girard, *Des Choses cachées depuis la fondation du monde* (Paris: Grasset, 1978) and Marie Balmary, *Le sacrifice interdit: Freud et la Bible* (Paris: Grasset, 1986).

11. See D. J. Hall, *Imaging God: Dominion as Stewardship* (Grand Rapids: W. B. Eerdmans Friendship Press, 1986), 135: "Calvary . . . , indeed, was and is so crucial an occasion that the mind and devotion of the devout is tempted to forget, in its grateful Christocentrism, that Jesus was not centred in Jesus at all. He is called the Christ precisely because of that."

12. Acts 4:12.

13. John 3:16.

14. Karl Kautsky, *Foundations of Christianity: A Study in Christian Origins*, trans. from the German by Jacob W. Hartmann (London: Orbach and Chambers, [1925]).

15. Whether ultimately tantamount to deviation or regression, this kind of Christian power is in another field equally denounced by Eugen Drewermann, *Wort des Heils, Wort des Heilung*, 3 vols. (Düsseldorf: Patmos, 1989–90); Drewermann, *La parole qui guérit* (Paris: Éditions du Cerf, 1991), 283: ". . . it is precisely the Old Testament which, fearful of the fertility religions, refuses to attribute to sexuality a divine sacramental character. And that is what I find astonishing in the Catholic Church: this idea that the encounter between man and woman is a means of approaching God. This is almost a falling back into the ancient myths."

16. Galatians 3:28. Cf. Colossians 3:11.

17. John Calvin, *Institutes of the Christian Religion* (Philadelphia: Westminster, 1961), 2.12.1. Cf. Galatians 4:2–11.

18. John 12:45, 14:9, 1:18.

19. Matthew 25:31–46.

20. Exodus 4:10–11.

21. Amos 3:2.

22. "Pleromatic" comes from the Greek *pleroma*, which means fulfillment or the fullness of time.

23. Rudolf Bultmann, "The Conception of Man and of the World in the New Testament and in Hellenism," *Theologische Blätter* 19 (1940); Bultmann, *Foi et compréhension*, vol. 1 (Paris: Éditions du Seuil, 1970), 457.

24. Anne Fremantle, *The Age of Belief: The Medieval Philosophers* (New York: Houghton Mifflin, 1954).

25. In a study on light and its symbolic role in paintings of the Middle Ages (with their golden background representing divine glory), and focusing on the work of Caravaggio, who departs even from the perspectivism of the Renaissance, Andrea Dall'Asta points out that in *The Calling of Matthew* "the character of Christ which occupies a central place in the [Gospel] narrative, finds itself in a zone of darkness: only his profile and his right arm are partly illuminated by the light. . . . The objects and the persons appear as emergences, as beings per se in their individuality, singularity and otherness" ("The Image of a God Who Passes By," *Recherches de science religieuse* 85, no. 3 [1997]: 352). "Christ shows himself as experiencing transitoriness. He is the one who passes by" (362). He "withdraws gradually from the world so that man achieves his freedom, and is free to recognize the tracks of his passage through history . . . in a world where he can live *etsi deus non daretur* [as if God did not exist]" (363).

26. Bultmann, *Theology of the New Testament*, vol. 2, §46.1.41.

27. Pelikan, *Jesus through the Centuries*, 10. For Herbert Braun, see his *God and Christ: Existence and Province*, Journal for Theology and Church, vol. 5 (New York: Harper, 1968).

28. Ernst Bloch, *Das Prinzip Hoffnung* (Frankfurt am Main: Suhrkamp Verlag, 1969 [©1959]), vol. 3, part 5, §53,ii, pp. 1493ff.

29. Bultmann, *Theology of the New Testament*, vol. 2, §46.1.

30. See Norman Perrin, *Jesus and the Language of the Kingdom: Symbol and Metaphor in New Testament Interpretation* (Philadelphia: Fortress Press, 1976), 158.

31. Hans Urs von Balthasar, *Word and Revelation: Essays in Theology* (New York: Herder and Herder, 1964), 1:71.

32. To my mind, the christological concentration and the positivism of revelation of which Barth is accused can also be rendered in this way.

33. Calvin, *Institutes of the Christian Religion*, 1.1.1.

34. We turn to Pascal and go beyond the theologically essential contribution of Luther, which is not negligible—far from it.

35. Blaise Pascal, *Pensées*, trans. W. F. Trotter, with an introduction by T. S. Eliot (New York: E. P. Dutton, 1958), fragment 526.

36. Ibid., fragment 525.

37. 1 Corinthians 2:8.

38. Calvin, *Institutes of the Christian Religion*, 4.17.30; see also 2.13.4.

39. François Wendel, *Calvin: Sources et évolution de sa pensée religieuse* (Paris: Presses Universitaires de France, 1950), 167.

40. Alfred Loisy, *L'évangile et l'église* (Paris: Picard, 1902; 5th ed., Paris: Emile Nourry, 1930), 153; see also 224.

41. Friedrich Gogarten, *The Reality of Faith* (Philadelphia: Westminster Press, 1968), 26–27; Gogarten, *Verhängnis und Hoffnung der Neuzeit* (Stuttgart: Friedrich Vorwerk Verlag, 1953; 2nd ed. 1958).

42. John Knox, *The Humanity and Divinity of Christ* (Cambridge: Cambridge University Press, 1967), 58. See Henry Slonimsky, "The Philosophy Implicit in the Midrash," *Hebrew Union College Annual* 27 (1956): 281: ". . . Messiah . . . is a supreme creation of religious genius, for it rests on two new religious insights, on two imperishable thoughts: first, that all men are one, and secondly that they have a future."

43. Psalm 19:1–4.

44. See Galatians 2:20.

45. Psalm 8:6; cf. Psalm 82:6; John 10:34.

46. Hebrews 2:17.

47. Cited by Maurice Goguel, *Jésus* (Paris: Payot, 1950), 49.

48. See Luke 1:35, 2:38; Romans 1:34.

49. John 20:25; 1 Peter 1:8; John 4:48. On the symbolism of the door, see Gabriel Vahanian, *La foi une fois pour toutes* (Geneva: Labor et Fides, 1996), 87–89.

50. John 14:2.

51. See Michael Theobald, "Le prologue johannique (John 1:1–18) et ses lecteurs implicites," *Recherches de science religieuse* 83, no. 2 (1995): 207.

52. John 1:18.

53. Vahanian, ed., *Le salut*. Cf. Bart D. Ehrmann, *The Orthodox Corruption of Scripture* (New York: Oxford University Press, 1993), 201, 202: "It is particularly important to stress that Luke has not simply overlooked or avoided making such references [to Jesus's atoning sacrifice]; he has gone out of his way to eliminate notions of atonement from the one source we are virtually certain he had before him, the

Gospel of Mark. Mark makes two poignant references to the salvific significance of Jesus's death, and Luke changes them both. The first and most obvious comes in the famous words of Jesus in Mark 10,45: 'For the Son of Man came not to be served but to serve, and give his life a ransom for many.' If Luke [18:27] found this theology acceptable, it is virtually impossible to explain why he omitted the verse altogether."

54. Rosemary Radford Ruether is even more straightforward in saying that such a christology could lead only to Auschwitz.

55. See 1 Corinthians 1:23; Galatians 3:28.

56. Acts 4:10–12.

57. Rudolf Bultmann, "What Alienates Modern Man from Christianity," mimeograph of a conference delivered at Syracuse University in 1959.

58. James 2:17.

59. In this idea of religious language I fall in line with Franz Theunis's proposals in "Zur Sprache des Glaubens," in *Weltgesprach: Sprache und Wahrheit* (Vienna: Herder, 1969), 16–31.

3. Fictions of Faith

1. Tying the distinction between story and scenario to the linguistic turn and the primacy of language, one could say that no story is told unless it becomes a scenario. In his comment on the quest of the Holy Grail, Tzvetan Todorov points out that, from one story to the next, the Grail stands for nothing else than the quest of a story that cannot be repeated. See Giorgio Agamben, "Face au cinéma et à l'Histoire: À propos de Jean-Luc Godard," *Le Monde,* October 6, 1995, xi: "Modernity comprises four thinkers of repetition, Kierkegaard, Nietzsche, Heidegger, and Deleuze. They all have shown that repetition is a return not to the identical but to the possibility of what has actually been. What returns returns as possible. Hence the proximity of repetition to memory: remembrance is the return of what has been so far as it was possible. Repetition is remembrance of what has not been. It is a definition of film as well—a remembrance of what has not been. That is, exactly the opposite of what the media are up to. . . . The fact they deal with cannot be repeated, and with regard to it we are powerless. This is the media's tyranny: it loves indignant—but powerless—citizens." See Todorov, *Poétique de la prose* (Paris: Éditions du Seuil, 1971), 223: "Art need not *represent* life or what's most essential to it, but must itself *be* life." See also Hans Georg Gadamer, *Wahrheit und Methode,* quoted by A. D. Hirsch Jr., *Validity in Interpretation* (New Haven: Yale University Press, 1967), 251–52.

2. Amos N. Wilder, *Early Christian Rhetoric: The Language of the Gospel* (London: SCM Press, 1964), 37, 66 (emphasis mine).

3. See Exodus 3:5; Joshua 5:15; Isaiah 20:2; Acts 7:33.

4. Fiction, according to *Webster's Collegiate Dictionary* (Springfield, Mass.: G. and C. Merriam Co., 1940), means "an assumption of a possible thing as a fact."

5. In an article titled "Religious Symbols and Our Knowledge of God," Paul Tillich writes: "[T]he materials in the Lord's Supper are symbolic. Now you will ask perhaps, 'only symbolic?' That sounds as if there were something more than symbolic, namely 'literal.'" *Christian Scholar* 38 (September 1955): 195.

6. Habakkuk 2:4.
7. Martin Buber. See also 2 Corinthians 13:5.
8. Genesis 2:19ff.
9. James 2:17.
10. Although in view of this desacralized ethics Bultmann speaks of the *Enweltlichung der Welt*, he also describes this as a process through which nature is rendered to itself.
11. While in *The Spiritual Situation of Our Technical Society*, ed. J. Mark Thomas (Macon, Ga.: Mercer University Press, 1988), Tillich deplores the denaturation of religion, elsewhere, at an earlier stage of his career when he publishes what becomes his *Écrits contre les nazis*, he clearly contends that the symbolic language to come could develop only in the concordance of religious symbolism with profane symbolism (see esp. 156).
12. The quest for identity evinces this trend and frustrates it at one and the same time as soon as it yields to the contention that, above and beyond their constituencies, minorities must be right. Only an ideological (i.e., remaindered) version of the social rhetoric is available to minorities imbued or favored with the politically correct know-how of majorities shorn of cohesion as well as coherence once the efficacy of their erstwhile meaning-giving center has been outgrown. In *The Quest for Identity* (New York: W. W. Norton, 1958), Allen Wheelis rightly argues that "modern man cannot recapture an identity out of the past, for his old identity was not lost, but outgrown: identity is not, therefore, to be found; it is to be created and achieved" (105).
13. Though from creation to fulfillment this vision of a world as God's own utopia is obvious in the eyes of Jesus, it is by his adversaries likened to a blasphemous, anarchic, misrepresentation of God's reign. They could only equate anarchy with blasphemy. As I have tried to show elsewhere, anarchy, viewed from a biblical perspective, could as well form a pair with hallowing and tie in with utopia and the eschatology of the kingdom of God or the New Jerusalem. On the connection between anarchy and utopia, see Robert Nozick, *Anarchy, State, and Utopia* (New York: Basic Books, 1974); and John D. Caputo, *Against Ethics: Contribution to a Poetics of Obligation with Constant Reference to Deconstruction* (Bloomington: Indiana University Press, 1993), 221.

4. The Death of God and the Ambiguities of the Secular

1. Scharlemann, ed., *Theology at the End of the Century*, 3, 4, 6.
2. On Kant and ontotheism or the end of metaphysics and secularization, see Alphonse de Waehlens, "La sécularisation dans la pensée de Heidegger," in *Herméneutique de la sécularisation*, ed. Enrico Castelli (Paris: Aubier, Éditions Montaigne, 1976), 295.
3. Scharlemann, ed., *Theology at the End of the Century*, 3.
4. Winquist, "The Silence of the Real," in *Theology at the End of the Century*, ed. Scharlemann, 14.
5. John 7:22–24 and 40–47.

6. Mark 1:14; Matthew 12:28; Luke 4:43.

7. Against this confusion of holy and sacred stands also Emmanuel Lévinas; see Jacques Derrida, *Foi et savoir, suivi de Le siècle et le pardon* (Paris: Éditions du Seuil/Points, 2000), 53.

8. See Samuel Beckett, *Waiting for Godot* (New York: Grove Press, 1954).

9. Tillich, *Écrits contre les nazis*, 156. In the same work, however, Tillich criticizes Barth for not admitting to the Christian background of secularism or to the Christian interpretation of the proletarian movement (see 180).

10. Paul Tillich, *Political Expectation* (New York: Harper and Row, 1971), 61.

11. In the following quotation from Tillich's *The Protestant Era* (Chicago: University of Chicago Press, 1948), 214, read "secularity" instead of "secularism" and the whole thing falls into place: "Nothing is less Protestant than the Catholic sanctification of a special philosophy, a special art, a special ethics. This is just the way in which the Roman Church tries to prevent secular culture from raising a protest against the ecclesiastical forms. But this is not the Protestant way. Protestantism considers secularism as a continuous, ever changing task for its formative power. There is no fixed, not even a classical, solution. There are preliminary affirmations, constructions, solutions; but nothing is final. The Protestant *Gestalt* of grace is dynamic and flexible."

12. Psalm 89:7; Isaiah 40:18.

13. Proverbs 18:21.

14. See Richard Rorty, *Contingency, Irony, and Solidarity* (Cambridge: Cambridge University Press, 1991), 21.

15. See Wilder, *Early Christian Rhetoric*, 98.

16. Jacques Ellul, *Les nouveaux possédés* (Paris: Fayard, 1973), 114: "On the contrary, these secularized societies present the same organization as did traditional societies, with a system relating the sacred, myths, religions to the well-ordered ensemble of a sacral world."

17. Ibid., 88.

18. Ibid., 90.

19. Ibid.

20. Jacques Ellul, *La subversion du christianisme* (Paris: Éditions du Seuil, 1984), 66: "The sacred is not identical with the religious. Schematically, I would say that the sacred largely spills over religious phenomena, and that religion is one of the possible translations of the sacred."

21. Alasdair MacIntyre, holding also that humility is a virtue of biblical origin, insists on pointing out that for Aristotle it is a vice. See his *After Virtue*, 2nd ed. (Notre Dame: University of Notre Dame Press, 1984), 177, 182.

22. Rorty, *Philosophy and the Mirror of Nature*, 3.

23. Richard Rorty, "Truth and Freedom: A Reply to Thomas McCarthy," in *Prospects for a Common Morality*, ed. Gene Outka and John P. Reeder (Princeton: Princeton University Press, 1993), 287.

24. Richard Rorty, *Lire Rorty: Le pragmatisme et ses conséquences*, ed. Jean-Pierre Cometti (Combas: Éditions de l'éclat, 1992), 167.

25. Richard Rorty, "Philosophes et romanciers," *Lettre internationale* (Winter 1990–91): 42–46: "a future imaginary society where no one dreams of believing that God, or truth, or the nature of things is on one's side. In this utopia . . . in this community, there would be nothing that would closely or remotely look like a state religion or philosophy."

5. The Secular and the Deregulation of Religion

1. Rorty, *Philosophy and the Mirror of Nature*, 38.

2. See, aside from Allen Wheelis quoted above, Thomas Luckmann and Peter Berger, "Social Mobility and Personal Identity," *Humanitas* 7 (1971): 1, 93–110; Charles E. Winquist, "Identity Is in the Making," in *Desiring Theology* (Chicago: University of Chicago Press, 1995), 40.

3. Rorty, *Contingency, Irony, and Solidarity*, 87 n. 8.

4. Ibid., 196.

5. Ibid., 198.

6. Ibid., 177.

7. Luke 10:30; Matthew 25.

8. Rorty, *Contingency, Irony, and Solidarity*, 198.

9. Karl Mannheim, *Freedom, Power, and Democratic Planning* (New York: Oxford University Press, 1950), 288. See also John 14:2.

10. Quoted by William G. McLaughlin, "The Diverse Origins of the American Tradition of Separation of Church and State," *Cimarron Review* 2 (1967): 50. In his *Ethics*, Dietrich Bonhoeffer underlines the differences between the American and the French revolutions and their consequences with respect to Christianity and its relation to democracy.

11. On democracy and desacralization, see Paul Tillich, *The Religious Situation* (New York: Meridian Books, 1956), 107–8.

12. Rorty, *Contingency, Irony, and Solidarity*, 60.

13. See W. D. Davies, *The Gospel and the Land: Early Christianity and Jewish Territorial Doctrine* (Berkeley: University of California Press, 1974); Davies, "La dimension territoriale du judaïsme," *Recherches de science religieuse* 66 (1978): 4.

14. Psalm 115:16.

15. John 16:17–33; Matthew 13:13–17; Luke 12:41; Mark 12:12.

16. In the quotation from John Cotton, the commonwealth encompasses the churches. In the Middle Ages, it was the church that encompassed nations and states. They exemplify two of the five approaches to the paradigmatic understanding of the relation between religion and the secular in the West: Christ dominating culture in the latter, and Christ transforming culture in the former, as described by H. Richard Niebuhr in *Christ and Culture* (New York: Harper and Brothers, 1951).

17. As I have tried to show elsewhere, in *God and Utopia: The Church in a Technological Civilization* (New York: Seabury Press, Crossroad, 1970), or in *L'utopie chrétienne* (Paris: Desclée de Brouwer, 1989), this utopian paradigm is to be distinguished from the sacral paradigm of religion. They correspond respectively to the Western and Eastern approaches and are here opposed only for the sake of

convenience. Actually, the distinction hangs on a matter of emphasis: utopia is present in every religion.

18. Acts 17:16–31.
19. See Martin Buber, *Between Man and Man* (Boston: Beacon Press, 1955), 80.
20. Philippians 2:5–8.
21. Acts 17:16–31; 1 Corinthians 8:4–6.
22. James Morrow's satirical novel *Blameless in Abaddon* (San Diego: Harcourt, Brace, Harvest, 1997) offers quite an apt description of this trend, in particular on 135, 171.
23. Paul argues as much about the church in Philippians.
24. Matthew 3:9.
25. Hebrews 13:14.
26. See Genesis 11:1–9.
27. This identification of religion with building bridges is echoed by the designation of the pope as *pontifex maximus*.
28. Or, likening a river's banks to the halves of a broken object, one is reminded of Pierre Emmanuel's insistence on the fact that there is no symbol and therefore no covenant except through language. "In its original sense, a symbol is the sign formed by bringing together the two halves of a broken object. As such, the object is nothing but itself: only putting it together is an act of language" (*Le goût de l'Un* [Paris: Éditions du Seuil, 1963], 51).
29. Whatever the difference, it slides into a split between us and them as it does between subject and object only by a language forgetful of the fact that "nothing—no being present and 'in-différant'—comes before [. . .] 'différance' and spacing [l'espacement]. No subject is agent, author and master of 'différance' and to whom 'différance' would hark back eventually and empirically. Subjectivity—like objectivity—is an effect of 'différance'. . . . Metaphysics has always consisted, as could be shown, in seeking to snatch a presence of meaning, under this name or another, from 'différance'" (Jacques Derrida, *Positions* [Paris: Éditions de Minuit, 1972], 40, 41).
30. Tillich, *Écrits contre les nazis*, 42. In the same work, Tillich criticizes Barth for not admitting to the Christian background of secularism or to a Christian interpretation of the proletarian movement (180).
31. Mircea Eliade, "Note pour un humanisme," *Nouvelle nouvelle revue française* 9 (November 1961). Eliade, however, sees no connection, though it be more decisive, between technology and the rise of this new type of religiosity. See Ernst Troeltsch, *Religion in History*, ed. James Luther Adams and Walter F. Bense (Edinburgh: T & T Clark, 1991); Vahanian, *God and Utopia*.
32. *Epistle to Diognetus* [*À Diognète*] 5–6, ed. H. I. Marrou, Sources chrétiennes, 33 (Paris: Éditions du Cerf, 1991), 62–63, as translated by Jaroslav Pelikan in *Jesus through the Centuries*, 49–50. Cf. Zechariah 14:20–21: "In that day shall there be upon the bells of the horses, holiness unto the Lord; and the pots in the Lord's house shall be like the bowls before the altar. Yea, every pot in Jerusalem and in Judah shall be holiness unto the Lord of Hosts; and all they that sacrifice shall

come and take of them, and seethe therein; and in that day there shall be no more the Canaanite in the house of the Lord of Hosts."

33. Saint Augustine, *Confessions* 10.6.

6. Worlding the Word

1. Saint Augustine, *Confessions* 11.14.
2. Ephesians 5:16; Colossians 4:5.
3. The binary implies a choice, dualism an opposition. They should not be confused.
4. From the Old Testament to the New Testament the Bible is haunted by the idea of time. And not only in the wake of Ecclesiastes, whose influence, in a supreme irony, still remains to be determined. The Bible itself keeps from objectifying time—and from slicing it up. In contrast with the word (*verbum*), the written word (*scriptum*), in order to last, must itself be ephemeral. Or else there would not be two testaments constrained, maintained, by one and the same word of God.
5. Genesis 35:9–15.
6. As is known, this formula for the radical otherness of God harks back to Saint Augustine, and recently to Kierkegaard and Ricoeur.
7. Time neither dies for us nor redeems us; we must on the contrary redeem time (Ephesians 5:26; Colossians 4:5).
8. Would the alternative of sin and grace have meaning if a believer were not at the same time sinful and justified (Luther)? At best, the dialectic of "already/not yet" is only a linear bastardization of the eschatic dialectic of the *et tamen*, which can also be rendered "in spite of" to the extent that, before God, a human being is at one and the same time sinful and justified—simultaneously.
9. Hebrews 13:14; Philippians 3:20.
10. Apocalypse is meant here in the sense of catastrophe and cataclysm accompanying the end of the world and not in the sense of St. John's Book of Revelation.
11. John 10:11.
12. Saint Augustine, *Confessions* 11.7.
13. The French *siècle* means, of course, century, but it also points to the worldhood of the world, as the German *Weltlichkeit* is often translated, though it also means secularity.
14. Saint Augustine, *Confessions* 13.36. To grasp the fundamental difference between the sacred and holiness and therefore the better to grasp the link between hallowing (sanctification) and secularization, one need only compare two French translations of Jeremiah 17:22, "Sanctify the Sabbath day" (Segond) and "keep it sacred" (TOB [*traduction œcuménique de la Bible*]).
15. Martin Heidegger, "Le concept de temps," *Cahiers de l'Herne*, no. 45 (1983): 27.
16. Paul Ricoeur, *Temps et récit* (Paris: Éditions du Seuil, 1985), 150.
17. Heidegger, "Le concept de temps," 36.
18. Ibid.

19. Matthew 16:17.

20. Mark 14:41; John 7:30.

21. Rudolf Bultmann, *The Presence of Eternity: History and Eschatology*, Gifford Lectures, 1955 (New York: Harper and Brothers, 1957), 37.

22. Ibid., 35.

23. Following Stanislas Breton, here we understand this term of "analysis" as being the ancestor of deconstruction.

24. Although objective, the past does not remain less ambiguous; we are determined by it but not to the point of having to renounce a certain capacity for decision (see Bultmann, *The Presence of Eternity*, 141), by virtue of which we are all at an equal distance from God, unhampered by our preconceptions; predestination is perhaps another way of saying this.

25. John 8:58.

26. J.-B. Pontalis, *Ce temps qui ne passe pas* (Paris: Gallimard, 1997), 22; see also 11–12.

27. Søren Kierkegaard, *L'école du christianisme*, trans. P. H. Tisseau (Bazoges-en-Pareds: Chez l'auteur, 1936), 27. In *The Great Code: The Bible and Literature* (London: Routledge and Kegan Paul, 1982), Northrop Frye suggests that no sooner does God speak and become the Word of God than God is sentenced to die.

28. See Saint Augustine, *Confessions* 11. I owe this idea of time as an extension to conversations with Maurice Boutin.

29. Ephesians 5:16; Colossians 4:5.

30. Jeremiah 33.

31. See Gregory of Nyssa: "It would be the object of lengthy research to know how that comes which . . . is always present." Quoted in Jean-Marc Saint, "Celui qui vient," *Renouveau*, December 7, 1997.

32. John 1:14.

33. Isaiah 40:6–7; Augustine, *Confessions* 1.3: "You fill all things, but do you fill them with your whole self? . . . Does this mean that one part of you is greater and another smaller? Or are you present entirely everywhere at once, and no single thing contains the whole of you?"

34. See Frye, *The Great Code*, 108.

35. Martin Heidegger, *Sein und Zeit*, 17th ed. (Tübingen: Max Niemeyer Verlag, 1993), 430–31.

36. Add to these the expression "as if." See 1 Corinthians 7:29–30; 2 Corinthians 4:7–11.

37. Calvin, *Commentaires sur le Nouveau Testament*, 4 (Toulouse: Société des livres religieux, 1894), 85.

38. James Barr, *Biblical Words for Time* (London: SCM Press, 1962).

39. See Vahanian, *La condition de Dieu*, and *No Other God*.

40. Romans 6:23.

41. Cicero, *De natura deorum* 1.34. Words, as Cicero shrewdly points out, are of themselves harsh but are softened by their use. See also Thorlief Boman, *Hebrew Thought Compared with Greek* (New York: W. W. Norton, 1970), 93.

42. Jeremiah 8:7; 1 Corinthians 2:7.

43. 2 Timothy 1:9.

44. Isaiah 43:10–12.

45. Isaiah 43:10; Amos 3:2; Matthew 12:18.

46. Acts 17:28.

47. Job 38:28.

48. Barth, *Die kirchliche Dogmatik*, vol. 1, part 2, §14.1, p. 57.

49. See Gabriel Vahanian, "En ce jour-là: La structure eschatologique de la liturgie," in *Temporalité et aliénation*, ed. Enrico Castelli (Paris: Aubier, Éditions Montaigne, 1975); Vahanian, "Pour une éthique des sacrements," in *Les sacrements de Dieu*, ed. Joseph Moingt (Paris: Recherches de science religieuse, 1987); and, in a minor mode, see also my proposal in *Renouveau*, March 2, 1956.

50. Barth, *Die kirchliche Dogmatik*, vol. 1, part 2, §14.1, p. 55. In his Gifford Lectures, 1947–48 (*Christianity and Civilization* [New York: Charles Scribner's Sons, 1948], 1:50), instead of incarnation, Emil Brunner even suggested "intemporation," whereas intemporalization is nowadays put forward by J.-P. Manigne, *Les figures du temps: Poétique de la foi*, vol. 2 (Paris: Éditions du Cerf, 1991). See also Michael Wyschogrod, "Seen and Heard Commands: Ethics and the Metaphysics of Time," in *Philosophie de la religion entre éthique et ontologie*, ed. Marco Maria Olivetti (Padua: Cedam, 1996).

51. Genesis 2:4.

52. Revelation 21:5.

53. Ecclesiastes 3:1.

54. Genesis 8:22.

Epilogue

1. The connotations of secularization have been negative mostly because of an inveterate deafness to the distinction between secularity (as advocated not only by the Reformation but also by the Middle Ages) and secularism (as advocated by lost souls of a misguided modernity). See Vahanian, *The Death of God*.

2. As is well known, Israel, like the surrounding nations, wants a king. But the instauration of kingship goes against the grain of Israel's notion of authority of which, at first, royal power is rightly sensed as being a sacralizing instance.

3. According to Exodus 33:20, "No one can see God and live."

4. John 14:9. See also John 1:18.

5. Estranging from each other the God of Israel and the God of Jesus, Marcion (95–161, or 115–68 are variant years) sketched his notion of a so-called alien God and insisted on Israel's historical relevance to the religion of Jesus, but he vehemently denied it any theological relevance. See Adolf von Harnack, *Marcion: Das Evangelium vom fremden Gott: Eine Monographie zur Geschichte der Grundlegung der katholischen Kirche* (Leipzig: J. C. Hinrichs'sche Buchhandlung, 1921; 2nd ed. 1924; reprint, Darmstadt: Wissenschriftlichen Gesellschaft, 1960); Gabriel Vahanian, "Une religion orpheline: Le christianisme selon Marcion," *Foi et vie* 104, no. 1 (2005).

6. 1 Corinthians 8:4–6.

7. Georg Christoph Lichtenberg (1742–99), *Schriften und Briefe 1, Sudelbücher 1*, ed. Wolfgang Promies (Munich: Hanser Verlag, 1968), L 953: "Ist denn wohl unser Begriff von Gott etwas anders als personifizierte Unbegreiflichkeit?" I owe this reference to Reine Lambret. Cf. Lichtenberg, *Aphorismen und andere Sudeleien*, ed. Ulrich Joost (Stuttgart: Philipp Reclam jun., 2003), 62 (L 737/953). In the same vein, for Rousseau, there is no dogma in Scripture, while Hegel castigates Protestant scholasticism.

8. Matthew 6:24–34.

9. Luther defines the believer as a Christ unto his or her neighbor.

10. Lichtenberg, *Schriften und Briefe*, J 371. Jesus, like any other human being, can only speak his mother tongue, as does a parrot. But unlike the parrot's, Jesus's mother tongue cuts a Christlike figure—that is, a language in the light of which no language, including my mother tongue, can fall so short of that figure as to be too literal for being symbolic. There is no need for me to be some parrot of Jesus. Unlike Jesus's or my mother tongue, the parrot's mother tongue is no language: it has no capacity for a metaphor, for the worlding of a word, or for overcoming the cleavage between the singular and the universal or between the religious and the secular.

11. Proverbs 18:21.

12. John 1ff. and 18:37.

13. The incarnation, for John, belongs to the "untemporal" (to Malraux's *intemporel*), to that which, however ephemeral, for the time being lasts forever, *in saecula saeculorum*.

14. See Gabriel Vahanian, "A Secular Christ: Against the Parochialism of East and West," *Korea Journal of Christian Studies* 45 (2006): 5–27; Vahanian, "The Secular as Christian Contribution to the East/West Dialogue," *Kiats Theological Journal* 2, no. 1 (2006): 123–38.

Index

Abraham, 7, 43–44, 54–55, 59–60, 62–63, 72–73, 95, 99–101, 103, 114–15
Adam, 19, 55–56, 91, 118
adiaphoron/adiaphoricity, xvii, 25, 30, 79
Agamben, Giorgio, 139n1
already/not yet, 109, 119, 144
Amish, the, 74
anarchy/theocracy (anarchic/theocratic), xv, 19, 23–24, 103, 123, 134–35n26, 140n13, 150n26
anthropology, 50–53, 131
apocalypse, 109, 144n10
Aristotle, 7, 87, 141n21
Aron, Raymond, 90–91
asceticism, 33–34, 150
Asta, Andrea dall', 137n25
atheism/theism, xiv, 1–2, 6, 19, 21, 42–43, 59, 97. *See also* monotheism; non-theism; polytheism
Athens/Jerusalem, xi, 2, 21, 23, 60, 96, 128. *See also* Jerusalem; New Jerusalem
Auden, W. H., 24, 74
Augustine, Saint, xvii, 21–22, 32, 102, 105, 108, 110–12, 133n4, 134nn17–21, 136n6, 144n1, 144n6, 144n12, 144n14, 145n28, 145n33

autonomy/autonomous, 6, 8, 19, 50, 54, 71–72, 73, 78, 103, 131
Balmary, Marie, 136n10
Balthasar, Hans Urs von, 51–52, 138n3
Barr, James, 122, 145n38
Barth, Karl, xvii, 40, 50, 114, 126, 136n2, 138n32, 141n9, 143n30, 146n48, 146n50
Bauman, Zygmunt, 135n28
Beckett, Samuel, 141n8
Beker, J. Christiaan, 136n39
Berger, Peter, 142n2
Bethel, 108
Bethlehem, 80
binary, 78, 102, 106–7, 109, 112, 144n3
Bloch, Ernst, 51, 137n28
Boman, Thorlief, 145n41
Bonhoeffer, Dietrich, 4, 14, 50, 75, 142n10
Bonnard, Pierre, 136n5
Bouillard, Henri, 40
Boutin, Maurice, 136n6, 145n28
Bradlaugh, C., xiv
Braun, Herbert, 50, 137n27
Breton, Stanislas, 134n7, 145n23
Brunner, Emil, 146n50
Buber, Martin, 16, 78–79, 87, 133n5, 140n7, 143n19

Buddha, 128–29
Bultmann, Rudolf, 49–51, 63, 94, 114, 118, 136n39, 137n23, 137n26, 138n29, 138n57, 140n10, 145n21, 145n24

Cain, 24, 113
Calvin, John, xv, 25, 33–36, 46, 52–54, 91, 96, 99, 122–23, 134n11, 137n17, 138n33, 138nn38–39, 145n37
Camus, Albert, 134n16
Caputo, John D., 140n13
Cassirer, Ernst, 33, 135n36
Castelli, Enrico, 140n2, 146n49
Castoriadis, Cornélius, 134n26
Catholic substance, 83
Charlemagne, 30
chosen people, 18, 45, 61, 70–71, 81, 96
Christendom, xiv; late, 66, 80
Christ of faith, 50–51; God/"man," 95; measure of all, 95
christology, 48–53, 62–63, 131, 139n54; christological centralism, 48, 50, 136n11
christomorphic, 131–32
christophoric, 131
church (social novation), 32–33; state, 89, 136n41, 142n10, 142n25; visible/invisible, 35–36
Cicero, 145n41
clergy (religious/secular), xiv, 99
Cometti, Jean-Pierre, 141n24
commonwealth, 18, 36, 93, 96, 142n16
compatibility/complementarity, 23, 39–40, 102
contingency, 40, 46, 78, 82, 94, 120
correlation, vii, 12, 85
Cotton, John, 36, 93, 96, 142n16
covenant, 20, 43, 61, 71, 94–96, 100, 114, 119, 143n28
Crockett, Clayton, 133n2
Cross, F. L., xiv
Cummings, E. E., ix

"Cur Deus homo?" 48. See also incarnation; time/timing; worlding
Cyprian, xvii

Davies, W. D., 142n13
death, 3, 43, 47, 54, 61–62, 74, 85, 95, 105, 111, 113–14, 117, 120–24, 131–32
death of God, 11–12, 16, 20, 29, 30, 43, 50, 79–89, 99; and the Bible, 37
deconstruction, 21, 30, 69, 76, 88, 145n23
Deleuze, Gilles, 139n1
democracy, 24, 25, 54, 91, 142nn10–11
Derrida, Jacques, 61, 88, 131, 141n7, 143n29
desacralization/secularization, 17, 19, 23, 34, 37, 38, 42, 53, 73, 86, 94, 111–13, 125, 127, 131, 134n8, 140n2, 142n11, 144n14, 146n1
desire, vii–ix, 36, 38, 93, 105, 110, 115, 120–22. See also ultimate/intimate concern/preoccupation
destiny/history, 3, 7, 16, 18–19, 21, 26, 27, 28, 31, 41, 44–45, 50–51, 56, 62, 66–67, 70–71, 74, 81, 94, 100, 105–6, 108–11, 113–16, 119–20, 123, 125, 126–27, 129, 136, 137n25
de Waehlens, Alphonse, 140n2
Dillenberger, John, 136n39
dissenters, 28
Drewermann, E., 137n15
dualism, 14, 17, 39, 78, 101, 109, 112, 144n3

Easter, 44, 63, 67, 114, 126
Ebeling, Gerhard, 136n39
Ehrmann, Bart D., 138n53
Einstein, Albert, 70, 74
Eisenhower, Dwight, 36
Eliade, Mircea, 17, 101–2, 143n31
Ellul, Jacques, 7, 79, 81–82, 86–87, 141n16, 141n20
Emmanuel, Pierre, 143n28

empty tomb, viii, 26, 29, 43, 61, 67, 70, 74, 97–98, 111, 114
eschaton/eschatic, viii, 3, 18–19, 22, 23, 45, 49, 52, 53, 63, 96, 99, 109, 114, 115–16, 117, 119–20, 125, 126–27, 144n8; eschatological imperative, 121
eternal/ephemeral, xii, xvi, 3, 5, 7, 9, 18–19, 22, 26, 42, 47, 56–58, 62, 74, 95, 110–17, 122, 132; secondhand eternity, 121; timing, 112, 113
ethic: gratuitous, 69; ethical/moral, 121; otherworldly, 120; unprecedented, 7, 65, 69
ethnocentrism/ethnicism/ethnicity, 92, 93

Feuerbach, Ludwig, 51, 53
fideism, 1–2, 22, 80
"final solution," 31, 89, 90, 116
final/ultimate vocabulary, 88–89, 90, 92, 94, 116
flesh, ix, xii, xvi, 1, 3–7, 9, 18–19, 22, 38, 40–46, 48, 50–52, 54–56, 58, 60–64, 65–67, 72, 79–80, 87–88, 95, 97–98, 103, 106, 111, 117–18, 120, 122–23, 125–26, 129, 131–32
Fremantle, Anne, 49, 137n24
Frye, Northrop, 145n34
fullness/fulfillment/pleroma(tic), 17, 19, 40, 49, 56, 63, 67, 95, 105, 110, 111, 113, 114–15, 124–25, 126, 132, 137n22, 140n13
fundamentalism, 2, 9, 15–16, 19, 31, 35, 80, 102
Funk, Robert W., 136n39

Gadamer, Hans Georg, 131, 139n1
Garden of Eden, 8, 44, 61, 91, 99, 100, 103
Geiger, Abraham, 59
genealogy, 62, 109, 111
Geneva (theocratic/anarchic), xv
genocide (history vs. memory), 105

Girard, René, 136n10
Gnosticism, 109–10
God (being/wording), 72, 130; anonymous, 75; nameless, 72, 74
Gogarten, Friedrich, 138n41
Goguel, Maurice, 138n47
Good Friday, 63, 67, 80, 114
Good Samaritan, 93
grace, viii, 4, 18, 20, 22–23, 28, 44–45, 47, 55, 57, 59, 111, 112, 123–25, 141, 144n8
Gregory of Nyssa, 42, 145n31
Grünewald, Matthias, 25

Hall, D. J., 136n11
hallowing (sanctification), 16, 22, 96, 102, 125, 144n14
Harnack, Adolf von, 146n5
Hartshorne, Charles, 116
Hegel, Georg Wilhelm Friedrich, 20, 35, 67–68, 79–80, 118
Heidegger, Martin, 35, 78, 86, 88, 112–13, 118–19, 131, 139n1
Henry, Michel, 63
Herberg, Will, 36
heteronomous/heteronomy, 6, 54, 71, 103
Hirsch, A. D., 139n1
Holl, Karl, 33
holy/holiness, xvi, 6, 17, 23, 81, 127; and otherness, 74; and the secular, 7, 12, 17, 19, 23, 36, 122, 127, 141n7
Holyoake, George Jacob, xiv
Homer, 7
hope, 9, 14, 34, 47, 69, 91, 96–98, 104, 107, 129
hospitality, 77–78
human being into being human, 3–4, 6, 8, 17, 20, 28, 39, 41, 44, 47, 52, 55–56, 59–60, 66–69, 92, 95, 100, 102, 113, 117–19, 124, 128, 130
humility, 57, 84, 87–88, 141n21

iconoclasm (iconoclastic), xv, 6, 8, 15, 17, 18, 19, 30, 45, 49, 56, 59, 103, 124, 129, 133n1 (intro.)
identity/identities, 12, 15, 17–18, 28, 41, 91, 102–3, 107, 122, 140n12, 142n2
immanentism, 29, 34, 60
incarnation, 3–7, 17, 19, 25, 29, 37–45, 49, 51–54, 56, 58, 59, 61–64, 67, 70, 79, 80, 108, 110–15, 121–24, 127–29, 132, 146n50, 147n13; as timing, 104, 110
"intemporation," 4, 123, 146n50
intratemporality, 112
I-Thou, 27, 70, 78, 79, 102

Jacob, 54, 72, 108, 123; and Esau, 123
Jaeschke, Walter, 134n8
James the Less, Saint, 32
Jaspers, Karl, 30, 68–69
Jerome, Saint, xvii
Jerusalem, xi, 7, 96, 143n32. *See also* New Jerusalem
Jesus of history, 50; divinized, 54; as a Jew, 124
Jew/Greek, 7–8, 17–18, 23, 28, 46, 49, 62, 95, 103, 114, 128–29
John, 50, 56, 63, 72, 132, 134n11, 134n17, 144n10, 147n13
Joyce, James, 28, 46
Judaism/Christianity, 7, 59–60, 63

kairos, xvi, 9, 58, 85, 114, 119, 122, 124, 126, 134n26
Kant, Immanuel, 35, 78, 140n2
Kato, Takashi, 134n22
Kautsky, Karl, 45, 137n14
Kierkegaard, Søren, viii, 9, 29, 39–40, 65–69, 80, 116, 139n1, 144n6, 145n27
kingdom of God, viii, 45, 70, 80, 95–96, 117, 121, 126, 131–32, 134n11, 140n13
Knox, John, 138n42
Kundera, Milan, 88

Lacan, Jacques, 15, 69, 77, 122
Lamb of God, 43, 97; lamb and wolf, 97
Lambret, Reine, 147n7
language/metalanguage, 78, 143nn28–29; and God, 2, 47, 64, 72; mother tongue, 130, 147n10; primacy of, 93; tongues, 76
Last Judgment, 7, 14, 18, 33, 46, 71, 93, 98
Le Goff, Jacques, 135n35
Lévinas, Emmanuel, 141n7
Lichtenberg, Georg Christoph, 129, 147n7, 147n10
Lichtenberger, François, xiv
lips into words, xii, 5, 40
liturgy, 20, 125
Livingston, E. A., xiv
Loisy, Alfred, 138n40
Lord's Supper, 70
Luckmann, Thomas, 142n2
Luther, Martin, xv, 14, 33–35, 53, 57, 62, 80, 93, 136n34, 136n39, 144n8, 147n9

MacIntyre, Alasdair, 141n21
MacLeish, Archibald, 16, 62
Mallarmé, Stéphane, 132
Malraux, André, 26, 27, 147n13
Mannheim, Karl, 93, 142n9
Marcion, 128–29, 146n5
Marion, Jean-Luc, 133n1
Maritain, Jacques, 84, 133n1
Marrou, H. I., 143n32
Mary, 31
McLaughlin, William G., 136n42, 142n10
Melanchthon, Philipp, xvii, 53
memory/hope, 81, 104–7, 110, 112, 121, 139n1; singular/universal, 108
metaphoricity, 70, 94
Middle Ages, xv, 3, 20, 31, 33, 35, 53, 74, 137n25, 142n16, 146n1
modernity, xiv, xv, xvi, xvii, 25, 73, 80, 88–89, 99, 146n1
Moingt, Joseph, 146n49

monism, 39, 102, 103, 109
monotheism, 59, 96–97
More, Thomas, 14, 74, 90
Morrow, James, 143n22
Moses, 47
Müntzer, Thomas, 74
Muslims, 99

Nazareth, 50–52, 63, 74, 80
negation/denegation, 87, 105, 126
New Harmony, 74
New Jerusalem, 5, 7–8, 14, 44, 49, 61, 63, 89, 96, 99, 103, 140n13, 143n32. *See also* Athens/Jerusalem
newspeak, 15
Niebuhr, H. Richard, 142n16
Niebuhr, Reinhold, 24, 92
Nietzsche, Friedrich, 29, 36–37, 78, 91–92, 131, 139n1
non-theism, 43
novum, 125. *See also* eschaton/eschatic
Nozick, Robert, 140n13

Ockham, William of, 31, 32
Olivetti, Marco M., 38, 40, 136n1, 146n50
one/many, 78, 93, 96, 102
ontotheism/ontotheistic, 49, 52, 78, 88, 97–98, 140n2
otherness/alterity, viii, 58, 74, 78, 87, 102, 107, 110, 122, 126, 137n25, 144n6
otherworldly/otherworldliness, 20, 21, 22, 25, 26, 28, 31, 33, 35, 36, 51, 120
Outka, Gene, 141n23

pain/suffering, 8, 47, 92–93, 95, 96, 97, 98
Pascal, Blaise, 42, 53, 57, 58, 96, 102, 138nn34–35
Paul, 5, 7, 18, 46, 54, 59, 62, 97, 119, 120, 123, 128–29; Saint, 25
Pelikan, Jaroslav, 135n33, 137n27, 143n33

Pentecost, 77
Perrin, Norman, 138n30
Peter, 11
Picasso, Pablo, 25
Pickstock, Catherine, 19, 134n15
Plato, 7, 108
pluralism/pluralistic, 11, 22–23, 25, 77–78, 83–85, 86–87, 102–3, 135n29. *See also* monism
polytheism, 19, 59, 96, 97
Pontalis, J.-B., 145n26
postmodern, 25, 30, 76, 80–99
predestination, 34, 115, 123, 145n24
Prometheus, 103
Promised Land (salvation/right to earth), 8, 95, 96, 121
Protestant principle, 82–83
Przywara, Erich, 134n17

Reeder, John P., 141n23
Reformation, the, xv, 3, 32, 33, 50, 146n1
religion: denatured, 8, 94; deregulated, 99
Renaissance, the, 33, 137n25
resurrection/history, 60–63, 67, 131
revelation, 31, 40, 125; final/transitory, 109, 110, 138n32
Richard, Jean, 134n26
Ricoeur, Paul, 70, 112, 144n6, 144n16
Risen One/Christ, 43, 60, 61, 67, 119, 131
Rorty, Richard, 3, 7, 81–82, 87–88, 91–94, 97, 134n25, 141n14, 141nn22–24, 142n1, 142nn3–6, 142n8, 142n25
Ruether, Rosemary R., 139n54

sacramental materialism, 35
sacred/profane, xv, xvi, 6, 12, 17, 30, 41, 84, 86, 87, 100–101, 112, 141n16, 141n20; vs. holy, xvi, 12, 81, 86–88, 101, 141n7, 144n14; and Jesus, 95, 116; and secular, xvi, 44, 68, 74, 79, 99, 100

saeculum, xiii; *aureum* (golden age), xiii; *'olam/aion/chronos/kairos*, 124; this world, xvi
Saint, Jean-Marc, 145n31
saints/heroes, 26–29
salvation, viii, 5, 7, 18, 23, 25–26, 34, 41, 43, 45–46, 48–64, 80, 88, 95–99, 119, 131, 136n39; changing worlds, 32, 36; from/by/of God, 5, 7, 18, 25, 46, 54, 59, 62–63, 80, 95–99, 119, 120; as obsession, 8, 62. *See also* worlding
scarcity/frugality, 33–34
Scharlemann, Robert P., 76–78, 80, 135n28, 140n1, 140nn3–4
Schleiermacher, Friedrich, xvii, 34, 80
scientism, 1, 2
secular, vii, viii, xi–xvii, 11; eastern religions, 127; *weltlich*, xvi
secularism, xiii, xiv, 2, 4, 9, 15–16, 19, 21–22, 35, 37, 80, 84, 103, 141n9, 141n11, 143n30, 146n1
secularity/*saecularitas*, viii, xiii, xiv, xvi, 35, 37, 42, 52, 73, 97, 99, 102–3, 117, 141n10, 144n13, 146n1. *See also* worldhood
secularization, xiv, xv, 16, 19, 23, 34, 37, 38, 42, 53, 73, 94, 111–13, 125, 127, 131, 134n8, 140n4, 144n14, 146n1; as expropriation, xvi
silence of God/real, 79, 82, 85
Simmel, Georg, 134n26
simulacrum/simulacra, viii, 98
Slonimsky, Henry, 138n42
Socrates, 70
solidarity, 34, 46, 48, 72, 91–92, 95, 102, 107, 117, 122, 128
space/time, 6, 41, 56–58, 63, 101, 107, 136n6, 143n6
story/scenario, xii, 69, 94, 96, 101, 108, 110, 135n30, 139n1

Tacitus, xiii
technology/technological, 8, 30, 48, 57, 73, 83–86, 102, 121, 143n31

Tertullian, xiv, xvii, 20–22, 32
Thanksgiving, 16
Theobald, Michael, 138n52
theocracy/anarchy (theocratic/anarchic). *See* anarchy/theocracy (anarchic/theocratic)
theodicy, 98
theonomy/theonomous, 6, 19, 54, 100, 103, 131
Thomas, Mark, 140n11
Thomas Aquinas, Saint, 22, 31–32, 73, 91, 102
Tillich, Paul, vii, viii, xvi, 3, 7, 8, 16, 34, 70, 81–87, 91, 114, 122, 130, 134n26, 136n39, 139n5, 140n11, 141nn9–11, 142n11, 143n30
time/timing, xii, xvi, 6, 9, 19, 41, 56, 58, 71, 74, 104–27, 144n4; accomplished/unaccomplished, 113; anachronistic/deconstructed, 115; appointment/dis-appointment, 106; being, 104; binary, 104; chronology/history/eschatology, 107, 109, 111, 114; fulfilled/fullness of, 19, 111, 113, 124; and history, 45, 127; linear/cyclic, 56, 58, 106–7, 109, 115, 125, 144n8
Todorov, Tzvetan, 139n1
tolerance, 91
Tower of Babel, 44, 61, 77, 100
transcendence/immanence, 3, 19, 38, 55, 63, 127–29
Treaty of Westphalia, xiv
Troeltsch, Ernst, 134n6, 134n9, 143n9
truth, 9, 16, 23, 31, 47, 70, 88, 89, 93, 129, 132, 142n25

ultimate/intimate concern/preoccupation, viii, ix, 18, 23, 29, 32, 40, 45–46, 68, 74, 83, 92–96, 98, 116, 125–26
Ulysses, 100
universal/singular, ix, xiii, 6, 29, 49, 66, 71–72, 77–78, 108, 126, 130–31, 147n10

unprecedented/without precedent, 3, 6–7, 69, 71, 104, 120–21
utopia, 8, 24, 32, 48, 61, 74–75, 88, 90–91, 93, 102, 117, 121, 134n26, 140n13, 142n25, 143n17; democratic, 89–92; ideology, 90; utopianism, 5, 24, 96, 99. *See also* Garden of Eden; New Jerusalem; Promised Land (salvation/right to earth)

verbum caro, xvii, 64, 144. *See also* incarnation
vertical/horizontal, 34, 51–52, 63, 79, 87, 100, 119–20
Virgil, xiii
virgin birth, 56, 61–62, 67, 111

Walzer, Michel, 26, 35, 136n40
Weber, Max, 33, 86
Weltlichkeit, xvi, 8, 144n13. *See also* secularity/*saecularitas*
Wendel, François, 54, 138n39
Wilder, Amos N., 69, 139n2, 141n15
Willis, Allen, 140n12, 142n2
Winquist, Charles E., vii–ix, 25, 79, 135n28, 140n4, 142n2
Wittgenstein, Ludwig, 70

words/word, xi, 58, 100, 109; concept, 116, 122; God, 13, 117; mirror of the Word, 123
world, xiii, 20, 70; come of age (secularized), 14; globalizing, xi; as God's utopia, 75; *mundus* (world/cosmos, *monde*, *Welt*, *Umwelt*), xiii, xvi, 20; vs. worlds, 48; world without end (*saecula saeculorum*/for ever/once and for all), xvi, 3, 9, 20, 26, 86; as word order, 69
worldhood, xiv, xvi, xvii, 8, 14, 25–26, 29, 31–32, 35, 42, 51–52, 61, 66, 68, 75, 79–80, 97, 100, 117, 119–20, 122, 127, 144n13
worlding, xi, 3, 5, 76, 79–81, 87, 95, 97, 107, 113, 116, 118–19, 121–26, 127, 129, 131–32, 147n10; secularization, xv; worlded, 4–5, 20, 38, 42, 47, 56, 70, 103, 120, 126, 135
worldliness/otherworldliness, xiv, xvii, 20–21, 25–26, 35, 42
Wyschogrod, Edith, 26, 28, 135n30, 135n32
Wyschogrod, Michael, 146n50

Zusiah, Rabbi, 71

STUDIES IN RELIGION AND CULTURE

Edmund N. Santurri
Perplexity in the Moral Life: Philosophical and Theological Considerations

Robert P. Scharlemann
Inscriptions and Reflections: Essays in Philosophical Theology

James DiCenso
*Hermeneutics and the Disclosure of Truth: A Study in the Work of
    Heidegger, Gadamer, and Ricoeur*

David Lawton
Faith, Text, and History: The Bible in English

Robert P. Scharlemann, editor
Theology at the End of the Century: A Dialogue on the Postmodern

Robert P. Scharlemann, editor
Negation and Theology

Lynda Sexson
Ordinarily Sacred

David E. Klemm and William Schweiker, editors
Meanings in Texts and Actions: Questioning Paul Ricoeur

Guyton B. Hammond
Conscience and Its Recovery: From the Frankfurt School to Feminism

Roger Poole
Kierkegaard: The Indirect Communication

John D. Barbour
Versions of Deconversion: Autobiography and the Loss of Faith

Gary L. Ebersole
Captured by Texts: Puritan to Postmodern Images of Indian Captivity

David Chidester
*Savage Systems: Colonialism and Comparative Religion in
    Southern Africa*

Laurie L. Patton and Wendy Doniger, editors
Myth and Method

Orrin F. Summerell, editor
The Otherness of God

Langdon Gilkey
Creationism on Trial: Evolution and God at Little Rock

Michael L. Raposa
Boredom and the Religious Imagination

Peter Homans, editor
Symbolic Loss: The Ambiguity of Mourning and Memory at Century's End

Winston Davis, editor
Taking Responsibility: Comparative Perspectives

John P. Burris
Exhibiting Religion: Colonialism and Spectacle at International Expositions, 1851–1893

Jeffrey W. Robbins
Between Faith and Thought: An Essay on the Ontotheological Condition

Michael L. Raposa
Meditation and the Martial Arts

John D. Barbour
The Value of Solitude: The Ethics and Spirituality of Aloneness in Autobiography

Roger Caillois
Pontius Pilate (reprinted edition)

David M. Craig
John Ruskin and the Ethics of Consumption

Clayton Crockett, editor
Religion in a Secular World: Violence, Politics, Terror

Greg Johnson
Sacred Claims: Repatriation and Living Tradition

Frederick J. Ruf
Bewildered Travel: The Sacred Quest for Confusion

Jonathan Rothchild, Matthew Myer Boulton, and Kevin Jung, editors
Doing Justice to Mercy: Religion, Law, and Criminal Justice

Gabriel Vahanian
Praise of the Secular